In this day and age of self-promotion and "me first" thinking, Carson Tinker is the exception. Through his many trials and tribulations following the April 2011 Tuscaloosa tornado, Carson not only became a better national champion football player, but a true beacon of light for the Tuscaloosa community and Crimson Tide fan base. In his book, Carson's commitment to "be a blessing" to others is inspiring and contagious.

Pat Williams
Senior Vice President, Orlando Magic
Author of more than eighty-five books,
including *Coach Wooden's Greatest Secret*

If you have "it," you can't hide it. If you don't, you can't fake "it." Carson Tinker showed just how deep "it" runs in his blood as he went through unimaginable personal tragedy during and after the Tuscaloosa tornado of April 27, 2011. View this storm through the eyes of someone who could have floundered, but rather chose to flourish because of his faith.

John Croyle
Founder and executive director, Big Oak Ranch
Former University of Alabama All-American defensive end
Author of *Two-Minute Drill to Manhood*

All of us at sometime or another are going to face tragedy and difficult circumstances. How Carson Tinker handled his tragedy is not only a great example of his faith but also shows the power of our magnificent God. Carson's story appeals to the young and the old, as well as the sports enthusiasts.

Tommy Bowden
College football analyst
Former head coach at Clemson and Tulane
Author of *Winning Character: A Proven Game Plan for Success*

A Season to Remember is a reminder that in order to be truly strong, one must become weak. When we find ourselves unable to bear the weight of sorrow and loss, we find that Christ is sweeter and more powerful than ever. Carson Tinker is living proof that there isn't a more powerful platform for the gospel than pain and suffering. Faith becomes real in the ears and eyes of those who see and hear the response of one who is suffering and grieving. This book allows the reader to understand why bad things happen and that peace only comes from a loving, merciful God.

Rick Burgess
Cohost of *The Rick and Bubba Show*
New York Times best-selling author

What an inspiring book on so many different levels! Carson's story is sure to inspire many through their own adversities and struggles to achieve their dreams and goals.

Mac Powell
Lead vocalist and songwriter for Third Day

When faced with the incomprehensible devastation that followed in the path of the Tuscaloosa tornado, Carson, even in the midst of dealing with his own personal sorrow, served as a quiet leader in the healing of our community and continues to serve unselfishly in many ways to all who have supported him.

Sarah Patterson
Six-time national champion
University of Alabama head gymnastics coach

A Season to Remember is a direct reflection of what Alabama football is all about: courage, conviction, confidence, will to fight, and faith. This book gives an insight into the life of Carson Tinker and what makes the University of Alabama a special place: its people. Roll Tide!

Jeremiah Castille
University of Alabama football team chaplain
Founder of the Jeremiah Castille Foundation
Former University of Alabama All-American defensive back

I have been an Alabama television meteorologist for thirty-five years; no day in my career will compare to April 27, 2011. Words can't describe the encouragement I received after reading this book. Carson's story is powerful, uplifting, and a beacon of hope during the hard times we all have to face in life. Read it, and get a copy for others in your family and circle of friends.

James Spann
ABC 33/40 meteorologist
Birmingham, Alabama

In the moments following 5:13 p.m. on April 27, 2011, thousands of citizens transformed themselves into heroes and truly became the images of God throughout Tuscaloosa. Carson Tinker is one such hero, and his profile in courage continues to inspire. Clearly, Carson's story illustrates that even in our darkest hour, there was always a confident hope.

Walter Maddox
Mayor of Tuscaloosa

During the aftermath of the April 2011 tornado outbreak in Alabama there were so many stories of tragedy. There were also so many stories of ordinary people who became heroes not just because of their actions that terrible day, but for their courage in the face of tremendous adversity. Carson is truly one of those heroes. He showed us that there is no difficulty that the people of Alabama cannot overcome when we work together and put aside our own agendas for the greater good.

Robert Bentley
Governor of Alabama

There are times in life when the world will tell you that you're done, you're toast, you're never going to make it. Carson Tinker had every chance to buy into that. But, he didn't. After the 2011 tornado ripped through Tuscaloosa, Carson was a shining star during his rehab, his recovery, and his national championship playing days. When Carson's back was against the wall, he committed himself to being the best he could be . . . and more. His work ethic was unmatched. His passion was off the charts.

The book you're about to read chronicles every single moment of his journey. Prepare to be blessed!

Scott Cochran
Director of Strength and Conditioning
University of Alabama Athletics Department

I call my brother, Carson Tinker, a walking miracle. His book *A Season to Remember* is more than a story about his life, Alabama football, or a football season. It's a reminder about our need for love from a family, a team, and a community. It's a reminder that if you get up and keep fighting, you will reach the top of many mountains. It's a reminder that at the end of it all, Jesus wins. Read it and be reminded!

Shaun Alexander
Former University of Alabama All-American running back
2005 NFL MVP, author of *Touchdown Alexander* and *The Walk*

A SEASON TO REMEMBER

FAITH IN THE MIDST OF THE STORM

CARSON TINKER

WITH TOMMY FORD

B&H
PUBLISHING GROUP

NASHVILLE, TENNESSEE

978-1-4336-8289-6

Published by B&H Publishing Group

Nashville, Tennessee

Dewey Decimal Classification: 234.2

Subject Heading: FAITH \ CHRISTIAN LIFE \ HOPE

Cover photo by Kent Gidley, UA/Crimson Tide Photos

2 3 4 5 6 7 8 • 18 17 16 15 14

Dedication

*To Momma, Daddy, Annie, Grammy and Granddaddy,
Mawmaw, and Michael Pope, thanks for being such
a blessing in my life.*

Contents

Foreword

by Nick Saban

One of the proudest moments I've had as a coach was when Carson Tinker and our 2011 team were recognized with the Disney Spirit Award at the ESPN Awards Show in Orlando. When we look back at 2011 years down the road, I'm sure people will remember the National Championship, but I think the way we rallied as a community to help one another after the devastation and tragedy from the tornado will be a memory that is just as prominent. The Disney Spirit Award represented that and is something we can all be proud of.

My message in our meeting with the players after the tornado was that when you are part of a team, you are not just part of the team on Saturday afternoons. We are all part of the team year-round, in good times and in bad. It was an opportunity for our players to go out and help the people that have supported this program for so many years. They are all part of our team at the University of Alabama and their passion and support plays a very important role in the success of the program. Our players took that to heart and the 2011 season meant so much to them because they were representing more than just themselves.

We always talk as a team that you are not defined by your circumstance or adversity; you are defined by how you respond to it and move forward. I don't know if anyone had to overcome more in that regard than Carson. Dealing with the loss of a loved one, dealing with his physical injuries, he had to decide what path he was going to take. From where he was laying in that hospital bed when we visited him after the tornado to the point in his life he is in now, it has been a remarkable journey. Through the tragedy of the tornado, Carson probably lost the most, but he has also given the most back. There's no question he has responded to what was a tragic circumstance to set an example in terms of the positive way he represented his family, the University of Alabama, and our football program in a first-class manner.

It was an honor to coach Carson during his career at Alabama, and I think you will appreciate his story as you read this book. He wasn't handed anything in his athletic or academic career. It took great perseverance to go from walking on, to earning a scholarship, graduating, and starting as the long snapper on two National Championship teams. That would be a great story in itself, but the most impressive part to me is the way he responded to adversity and had a positive influence on so many people in so many ways.

Nick Saban, Head Coach, Alabama Crimson Tide

Prologue

Just moments before the tornado's fury hit a nearby city, causing several deaths, uprooting lives, destroying neighborhoods, and leaving kids without schools to attend, it blew right over us.

At least that's what I'm told today.

Golf ball-sized hail pounded down on cars. High winds knocked out power at the main hospital. But thankfully the generators kicked in, giving much-needed life to lights and sensitive medical equipment.

Hospital patients—including newborns and their mothers—were rolled into the hallways for safety. It was a time of despair and uncertainty, a time to acknowledge the brevity of life.

Of course, I don't remember anything about that tornado on Wednesday, November 15, 1989, the day I was born at Decatur (Alabama) General Hospital.

I do, though, remember the Tuscaloosa tornado of April 27, 2011, and how it forever changed the lives of countless numbers of people.

I just happen to be one of them.

I love Tuscaloosa. I love the University of Alabama. I love the fans, the students, and the community. They will always hold a special place in my heart.

That's why I've written this book. I don't want it to be about Carson Tinker; I want it to be about the love, companionship, relentlessness, perseverance, and triumph this community has shown me throughout my difficult times and how I've been blessed by it.

I also want this book to be about being a blessing, about people I didn't even know who reached out to me and had a tremendous impact on my life. They include people just like you, people who taught me that no matter what you're going through, you can get through it. I want to show you how God can use anyone, whatever you do and wherever you are, and help you accomplish things for His kingdom.

I've said from day one that I'm just a single story. Countless people were in the same circumstances as me, yet we all came together in perseverance and faith and rose back. This book is for people who are going through the toughest part of their lives and are fighting as hard as we did to recover—or who perhaps are having a hard time seeing much point right now in trying, who don't really see a future for themselves anymore. I went through a tornado, but everyone goes through storms of some kind. I want to tell you how God took me from the darkest part of my life and used it for good.

I poured my heart into writing these words. My emotions are real. I hope, no matter where you are in life, you'll walk away with something that will help you deal with your own struggles.

Folks in the Tuscaloosa community rose for the occasion when I needed them the most, and this is one small way of giving back to them. This book is my thank-you to the countless people who reached out to me and had such a positive influence on my life.

Second Corinthians 1:3–4 says that God, "the Father of mercies and the God of all comfort . . . comforts us in all our affliction, so that we may be able to comfort those who are in any kind of affliction, through the comfort we ourselves receive from God."

I've received so much help and blessing from Him in so many ways and through so many people. I just hope something I say is a blessing to you, so that you (and I) can go out and be a blessing to others.

CHAPTER 1

April 27

I try not to think about April 27, 2011, but I can't help it.

For everyone in the Tuscaloosa area and most of Alabama, this date will always be one of those "where were you?" moments instilled in our minds and hearts forever—the same way people of earlier days can recall where they were when they first heard about President Kennedy being shot, or when Neil Armstrong made his "one small step" on the moon, or when the space shuttle *Challenger* exploded over the Atlantic Ocean less than a minute and a half after liftoff.

For me, one of those watershed moments was in the sixth grade at Brookhaven Middle School in Decatur, Alabama, the day when terrorists flew planes full of passengers into the World Trade Center towers and the Pentagon on September 11, 2001. I was standing outside a coach's office and noticed how upset all the teachers had become. I didn't really know what the World Trade Center was. We had televisions in all the classrooms, and every channel was airing some kind of news about it all day long. I remember it like it was yesterday.

As memorable as these types of moments are in our lives, we experience most of them as spectators. They unfold before our eyes on television. Rarely are we eyewitnesses or active participants in the events.

For the April 27 tornado and its aftermath, however, I did much more than watch from the sidelines. I was in the game, an unwilling participant in an event that—in only a few seconds—would reorient the rest of my life.

Early that morning, Tuscaloosa got a foreshadowing of what was to come less than twelve hours later. Around 5:30 a.m., roaring thunder rattled our windows and shook my little four-bedroom house, located a couple of miles from the University of Alabama campus. I sprang up in bed, not sure what was hitting us. I peeped out my window and saw enormous streaks of lightning illuminating the black sky.

But—OK, so it was storming. So what?

I looked at my phone to see what time it was, then went back to sleep, trying to get as much rest as possible before needing to be up for my 8:00 class. My alarm went off a little more than an hour later. I got dressed and was off to school, just like any other day. Of course, I assumed the bad weather had passed, even though the forecasters—and my mom via text message—insisted more was on the way.

I was a junior majoring in marketing. Just a normal college student. Sure, I had played on the Alabama football team for the previous three years, had just finished my first year as a starter, and had been on the BCS Championship squad in 2009. But I wasn't a marquee player, just the long snapper. (Most people don't even know what a long snapper is—the guy who snaps the ball on punts and kicks.) I wasn't a top wide receiver recruit with countless offers from all over the country. I was just an average guy who was pretty good at throwing a ball backwards between my legs. And most of my closest friends weren't even football players.

I tell you this because while I was at Alabama, I always considered myself just an ordinary person that anybody could relate to. I wasn't famous. Not many people knew who I was or knew I played football. I wasn't on Facebook, didn't have a Twitter account. I was low-key and I liked being that way.

Once I got to campus that morning, I met up with some friends, and we filed into our Consumer Behavior class, followed an hour later by our Professional Selling class. After that, I was done for the day. And since it was late April—one of the few times of year when we could take a small hiatus from football—I headed back to my house to relax.

I always loved driving through campus on my way home. I usually got caught in traffic, but it was worth it. That was a part of it. I loved the campus, the people, the tradition, and everything associated with it. I'd drive by the stadium and see everyone walking to class, talking to their friends. I'd go past Denny Chimes, the big bell tower on campus, and usually see a few alums looking at the handprints and footprints of all the great team captains at Alabama. People would be lying around on the Quad under the big, beautiful trees, almost like they were stretched out at the beach. I loved all of that.

From there, I'd keep driving toward my house, past all the local businesses, most of them sporting some kind of sign or poster in their window supporting the University, saying "Roll Tide!" If you've ever driven through Tuscaloosa, you know what I'm talking about. There's a sense of pride in the community you can't put into words.

I pulled onto my peaceful 25th Street and drove down to my house, glancing across at the huge field I loved so much, where I'd so often go out with my two dogs. In fact, just as I was driving up, my roommate was letting them out of the house—Josey, the German shepherd, and the black Lab we just called B. They ran to the edge of the field, stopped in front of the gate, and looked back at me, waiting for the go-ahead to run out there.

"Not yet," I told them, and we all went inside.

By then, my girlfriend Ashley Harrison had arrived. The early morning storm had freaked her out, so she wanted to hang out at the house for the rest of the day. We were in what's called "dead week," the week before finals when professors aren't supposed to give exams. I don't think Ashley had a class until that evening.

The previous Sunday, Ashley had attended church with us at Shades Mountain Baptist in Birmingham. Her Catholic background didn't adequately prepare her for a good ol' Southern Baptist Easter service. It was, let's say, a little loud and rambunctious for her taste. I told her that's what heaven was going to be like, and we got a good laugh out of it.

After church, we had gone over to eat at my grandparents' house and had brought the leftovers back to Tuscaloosa with us that afternoon. Three days later, there we were at my house, eating the last little bit of ham, sweet potato casserole, grape salad, and Ashley's famous potato salad, which is the only potato salad I've ever liked. I was sad to see all the leftovers gone.

Shortly after lunch, probably around 1:00, Ashley started watching *The NeverEnding Story,* a kid's movie she had always liked as a little girl. She was mesmerized by it, but honestly, I thought it was pretty boring. So at one point, I decided to take Josey and B out to the field across the street and hit some golf balls.

After letting them run for a little while, I walked to the other end of the field to let out Saban, our neighbors' German shepherd, so that all three dogs could have some good playtime together. (I don't think I need to tell you how he got his name.) Saban just wasn't himself, though, for some reason. I remember noticing how agitated he was. Usually he and Josey and B would run around like crazy, but on this day things were different. He seemed anxious, like something was about to happen. You could tell he was on full alert, sniffing everything and acting strange.

By the time I got back to the house, Ashley had finished watching her movie. And for the next couple of hours or so, we worked outside, building a flower bed I had started around the entire house. A few weeks earlier, something had gotten into me—I don't know what—but I got on this beautification kick. I cleaned up the yard, pressure-washed the house, and got it ready to paint. Building the flower bed was just the next step in making our house one of the best looking in the whole neighborhood.

But the sky—I noticed it was starting to look bad again. Real bad.

Tornadoes, we heard, were touching down all over the state. Forecasters were saying there was a chance of one hitting the Tuscaloosa area as well. But we weren't worried. You never really believe that one might actually be coming your way. You just always think it's going to head another direction.

My next-door neighbor popped out of his house and started talking to us. I was kinda laughing about the weather, asking him if he was getting ready for the storm. "Naw," he said, "I'm leaving actually. Heading down to my place in Mobile." Pointing up to the two huge pine trees in his front yard, each at least fifty to sixty feet tall, he said, "See those trees? If a really bad storm comes through here, I'm afraid they're gonna fall on my house. They'd be the first thing to go. So I'm getting out of here."

It wasn't long after that—probably around 4:45—when the wind really started kicking up and the rain began coming down. Ashley and I headed inside. I decided to take a quick shower and then unexplainably put on a bathing suit and a T-shirt. Why the bathing suit, I don't really know. I just did. My roommates were laughing at me, "Hey, Carson, where's the pool, man?"

By this time, everybody was glued to the television— Ashley as well as my roommates, Payton Holley and Alan Estis. A skycam from downtown showed a massive, half-mile to mile-wide tornado headed in Tuscaloosa's direction, but from this report we thought it was going toward the Skyland Boulevard area, well south of our neighborhood.

Of course, curiosity got the best of us. Who doesn't want to venture outside to watch a big storm, see how close it is? It's kind of exciting, in a way. So Payton and I walked out onto the front porch. Glancing upward, we saw nothing but an eerie, dark, gray-greenish sky. Even with the knowledge of a tornado bearing down on Tuscaloosa, I still didn't believe it would hit us.

If I had thought we needed to take precautions, I know Ashley and my roommates would've trusted me. If I had said, "I think we might ought to leave now," that's what we would've done, no questions asked. In fact, we had always said if a tornado ever did come our way, we'd break into the vacant house next door and huddle in the basement. Nobody lived there, so it wouldn't have been a big deal.

But I didn't say anything.

And that's something I have to live with.

I felt like I was invincible, not in the sense that the house would protect us from harm, but because tornadoes only show up on the news, not on your front doorstep. That's just the way it goes. That's the way you think, if nothing like that has ever happened to you before.

We'll be all right. Don't worry.

While Payton and I were still out on the porch, my grandfather, Jim Cartledge, called my cell phone: "Carson, you need to get in your house, son. Promise me you're getting in a closet *now*!"

"Granddaddy, we're fine," I said, "We're gonna be OK." After all, our power was still on. That was a good sign. Couldn't be too bad, right?

Then, with a tone in his voice I'd never heard before—and hope I never hear again—he said, "Carson, I'm serious! Get in your closet now!"

I guess everybody's parents were watching the same report as my grandfather because by that time Ashley, Payton, and Alan were all on their phones. Parents were calling in a panic, telling us to get down, to go huddle up in a safe place. Obviously they knew more about the weather situation than we did, and for the first time we collectively realized: *OK, this is serious.*

We made a split-second decision to go into Alan's walk-in closet rather than break into the house next door. Alan's closet, I'd guess, was about seven feet wide and four feet deep. Definitely not made to fit four people. Ashley and Alan got in first, loyally followed by Josey and B, then me. Payton squeezed in last and closed the door behind him.

As scared as the others were, I still had that feeling of invincibility, as if this tornado—if there really was one—would just skip right over us. With four people and two dogs crammed into this tiny space, I tried my best to lighten the mood and make everybody laugh. This went on for about a minute.

Then the power snapped off.

Darkness.

Tension.

Shallow breathing.

Quiet.

And then . . . the furthest thing from quiet.

Before we felt it or saw it, we heard it. I remember thinking, *Wow, it really DOES sound like a train, just like everybody always said.* But the whole time, I'm still thinking it'll all be over in a few minutes: *It's not going to hit us; it's not going to hit us . . .*

But the noise level was increasing by the second. Then the house started shaking. We heard popping, rumbling, cracking, loud booms. Finally, I realized it was for real.

I grabbed Ashley and held her tight. I kept telling her, "It's gonna be OK; it's gonna be OK. We're going to be OK."

I remember her saying, "Carson, I'm scared."

Again, I tried to ease her anxiety by making her laugh.

The last thing I remember is her laughing.

We heard the house cracking and coming apart, windows crashing, walls tumbling. Then, just like that, the roof was ripped off right over our heads, and the darkness of the closet was suddenly flooded with gray, rainy daylight. I could feel us being picked up. It was like having one of those dreams where you're falling, except just the opposite. Falling up. I held on to Ashley with all my might as we were sucked out of the house.

The next thing I remember is standing some seventy-five yards away, across the street in the field, screaming Ashley's name.

Exactly what happened in between—or how much time had passed—I'll never really know.

CHAPTER 2

Growing Up Crimson

Just as a tornado welcomed me into the world in November 1989, the Tuscaloosa tornado of April 2011 just about took me out of it.

The one that churned directly over Decatur on the day of my birth—when I was less than three hours old—moved northeast from our location and touched down nearly twenty miles away at Redstone Arsenal in Huntsville. Hopping over to the busy Airport Road area, it took out eighty businesses, three churches, a dozen apartment buildings, and more than a thousand cars. Then it hit the Jones Valley area, destroying 259 homes and demolishing Jones Valley Elementary School. Although school had been dismissed a couple of hours earlier, thirty-seven students and five teachers were still in the building for their extended day-care program. Teachers moved the children from the second floor to a stairwell on the lowest floor. When the storm struck around 4:35 in the afternoon, several painters working in the nearby teachers' lounge ran in and, along with the teachers, shielded the children with their bodies.

Just think about it. Those kids are now in their thirties, probably married and raising families. Some are probably still in the Huntsville area and may even drive past the rebuilt

Jones Valley School location every day, a constant reminder of the time they were saved by brave men and women—the day someone else was a blessing to them.

In all, the Huntsville tornado killed twenty-one people, injured 463, and caused $100 million in damage. Back then, it was called an F-4, based on the Fujita Tornado Intensity Scale. Today, they would call it an EF-4. The "E" came along a few years ago and means "Enhanced."

My mom has told me about that day many times. She kids me about coming into the world with a bang—all eight pounds and twenty-one inches of me. She recalls being in labor during the chaos and not being able to get a room until later that night.

I know that God was looking out for us that day. Maybe, just maybe, it was because He had something bigger in store for me some twenty-one years later, when another tornado would come rolling into my town.

———————————

People ask me if I remember when I first became a Crimson Tide fan. Well, I'd have to say my entire life. I've always known how dedicated and loyal the Alabama fans are. I grew up in an Alabama household. I was saying "Roll Tide" in my baby stroller just like so many little kids I see today.

I remember riding next to my teammate Dont'a Hightower one time on the way to Fan Day, where thousands of folks come out for autographs and to watch the team scrimmage in Bryant-Denny Stadium. Everywhere we looked, little boys were dressed in full Alabama football gear, the little girls in Alabama cheerleader outfits. Dont'a said something like, "Man, these Alabama fans sure do love their team. They love Alabama." I didn't have the nerve to tell him that I was one of those kids once. I didn't want him and my other teammates to give me a hard time.

But it's true.

I'd always loved Alabama.

Growing up, I loved playing baseball. I was like many kids with dreams of one day playing in the big leagues. I played almost all the infield positions and even pitched a little and loved it.

I can still remember when I was about four or five, getting ready for T-ball. My dad and I went to the store to buy my first baseball glove. It was all black with the World Series trophy etched into the palm. I can remember us coming home and going right out into the front yard, doing my best to catch his underhanded throws. If I caught it, I'd take one step back. If I dropped it, I'd scoot one step forward. It was the first time I'd ever done anything in team sports.

And it was the first of many times for my dad and me to throw baseball in the front yard. We did it every night. He'd come home from work, and I'd be waiting on him with both of our gloves in hand. We'd throw until past dark, which probably wasn't too wise. I got hit in the head so many times my bruises looked like baseball seams. I always thought that was funny.

My mom would even come out there sometimes. She'd play catch, too, but it never really registered with me that she was a woman and that I didn't need to throw the ball to her as hard as I could. But she would catch it with the best of them . . . until she finally decided it might be better if she was the batter instead. She eventually became afraid I'd hurt her with my hard throws.

I was pretty good at baseball. I made All-Stars every year but one, and I took a lot of pride in being the best I could be. I always wanted to make my parents happy. Not in a sense that I wanted to gain respect from them, like I feel many kids do, but just because I loved seeing them with smiles on their faces.

They invested so many of their resources into my playing baseball—time, money, energy, and whatever else they could offer. My dad was always the coach, and my mom was always the team mom. They loved being up at the fields and being involved with my life. My dad always tried to pick my friends for our teams.

But he was more concerned with us having fun than with winning. Don't get me wrong—we were very competitive—but no doubt our teams always had the most fun. Looking back, that's what I remember the most. I don't remember our record from any year, nor can I remember any real details of the individual games. But I sure can remember how much fun I had playing baseball with my friends and my dad being the coach.

However, he did hate one particular thing I picked up as a baseball player: becoming a fan of LSU and their head coach, Skip Bertman. I wasn't necessarily a die-hard LSU fan or anything, but I just loved watching them play baseball. They won the NCAA championship in 1996, 1997, and 2000, and I just gravitated toward them because they were winners.

So sports was already becoming a huge part of my life. Besides baseball, I played basketball, soccer, and even took karate for a few months, earning my orange belt. My parents were always there for me, cheering me on, being involved. I played because I loved it, but what I love most about it now is that they enjoyed it so much. I feel like I was able to be a blessing to them through sports, even as a young kid.

Church was also a major part of my life growing up. I don't remember a time when we weren't worshipping on Sundays and Wednesdays at Central Baptist in Decatur.

When I was eight, I attended a "Singing Christmas Tree" performance at our church. I was mesmerized by everything I saw—the lights, the sounds, the music, the stage, and especially the tree itself. I was amazed at how our choir members could get up and down in it. Everything in the performance that night pointed to Jesus Christ as being our Lord and Savior. And on the way home, I began asking my parents all sorts of questions about Jesus. They answered every one.

Lying in my bed that night, I prayed and asked Jesus to come into my heart. I knew—even at eight years old—a void was in my heart that only Jesus could fill.

A few weeks later at my baptism, my mom's parents gave me a Bible as a keepsake from that special day. Fortunately, when the tornado ravaged Tuscaloosa, that Bible was at my parents' house.

When I was in the third grade, my mom found out she had ovarian cancer. I didn't know what all of that meant really. I just knew she was severely sick. They had caught it early, but she still went through two surgeries and seven months of chemo treatments. At the time of diagnosis, I think her survival rate was only about 20 percent. It didn't look good.

Yet both of my parents thought it was important to keep things as normal as possible around the house. They didn't want people bringing food in because they didn't want me to think she was too sick to cook. Despite her going through her treatments, you would never have known that anyone was sick at home. She still cooked, kept the house, and displayed a never-quit attitude.

A couple of weeks after my mom's first chemo treatment, her hair started falling out, which was hard for me to take. I didn't realize this was going to happen. It was very difficult for me to see. So as a way to lighten up the moment a bit, she came up with an idea. It was getting close to baseball season anyway, the time of year when I'd always get my head shaved. So after she gave me my summer buzz cut, she let me shave her head too. As serious as it was, we actually had a fun time with it. You can imagine how entertaining it was for a third-grader to shave his mother's head.

My mom never wore a wig. It never bothered her that people knew she had cancer. Everybody said she had such a pretty round head. People would compliment her on how good she looked bald. I really got a kick out of that—as if my haircutting skills really had anything to do with it.

While continuing with baseball, I also started playing football in the fifth grade. The only time I had played before then was flag football in a community league when I was six years old, but I hated it. The very first day of practice, a big kid busted me in the nose, and I wanted to quit, right there on the spot. I said I would never play football again.

My parents, however, told me I couldn't quit. They said football was a team sport, and I couldn't quit a team sport. They told me I'd have to finish what I'd started.

You learn life lessons at all sorts of ages, and this particular episode was one of the first big lessons I remember. I didn't realize it at the time, but the way my parents handled the situation and what they expected of me instilled a never-quit attitude that would later define me in everything I do. Looking back on those days, I'm glad they made me tough it out at a time when I didn't want to. I have no doubt this moment in my childhood helped prepare me for much larger tests down the road.

But once that season was over, I was ready to put football aside for good. And I did—for four years, until fifth grade—when some of my friends talked me into playing for the River City Youth Football league in Decatur. I had matured a lot since my bad experience the first time, and I now realized that football could really be enjoyable. I had also hit a growth spurt and was a lot bigger than most kids my age. That didn't hurt my desire to play either.

Our team, the Bears, was a solid unit that ran the triple-option. I must say that we were impressive, even for a bunch of ten- and eleven-year-olds. I played defensive end and fullback and, coincidentally, wore number 51, the same number I later wore for the Crimson Tide. We were the second-best team in the league both years I played.

If you know anything about organized youth football, you know about the one team that's just stacked every year. Well, in our league, it was the Chiefs. We didn't know a single one of those kids or where they came from. The first time we played them, they killed us. We had never seen guys so big that were supposedly the same age as us.

So to get ready for the Chiefs the next year, we conducted a few off-season workouts designed just for them. And when we played them again, it was a much closer game, with the lead changing back and forth the whole time. But on their last possession, they ran the ball behind their enormous line to score the winning touchdown. Even though they'd beaten us, we'd taken them to the wire.

In the seventh grade, I started playing for Brookhaven Middle School. Brookhaven was an eye-opening experience in my life that really helped me become the man I am today. I went from being at a magnet school where things like freedom and creativity were the focus to a school that really emphasized discipline and structure.

At Brookhaven, I played tight end and defensive end. But one of my coaches, Jerry Lindsey, began to teach me how to snap the football. I'd never tried doing that before—and probably never would have tried it if he hadn't introduced me to it. But I liked it. And I was pretty good at it.

I sure owe him a lot for that.

But even in developing a good understanding of the game, as well as getting an initial taste for long snapping, I mostly enjoyed playing football for the social aspect. I was able to be with my friends. Many of these guys I still call friends today. I looked at my teammates as my brothers. I once invited sixteen of them to come spend the night at my house. I was the only white kid. I guess you can say I developed color blindness at a young age.

During my time at Brookhaven, I began to learn that football was more than just a sport; it was a lifestyle. Things like discipline, character, commitment, pride, brotherhood, family, and hard work became more than just words to me. Our coaches instilled these traits in us not only on the field but also in the classroom. There was the time, for example, when I forgot all about a class project that was due. I hustled and did it that morning at school and turned it in later that day. Mine was just as good, or better, than anyone else's, but my teacher knew it wasn't my best. She went next door and showed it to Coach Lindsey.

Coach called me into the hallway, looked at my project, and asked if it was the best I could do. I said "No sir," and he immediately agreed with me. We both knew it wasn't. He then went on to tell me something I'll never forget. "Carson," he said, "you're a part of the majority of this population; you're one of millions of other people just like you. If you don't do something to separate yourself from them, you will never be anything special. You're an intelligent kid, but if you don't try your hardest at everything you do, you'll get lost in the shuffle of things. You have to give your all in everything you do, be special, make a name for yourself."

Believe me, that has stuck with me.

Coach Lindsey was *the man*. He had said what he did because he cared about me. I really appreciate him, not only for working with me every day and teaching me to snap the football, but for the lessons of life he taught me.

Brookhaven taught me the value of hard work and discipline, what character was all about. And I would need those core values to help me get through the next setback.

My *dad's* cancer.

_____

My mom and I were running some errands one day when, out of nowhere, she told me that my dad was sick. I remember exactly where we were. She said he had gone to the doctor and found out he had cancer, a melanoma that had spread to his lymph nodes.

Even though I was only twelve, I was a lot more mature then than when my mom developed cancer, so I knew what we were in for. She began to tell me what was wrong with him and the medical side of it. I remember I cut her off and simply asked if my dad was going to be OK.

She teared up and said, "I don't know, Carson."

Neither one of us said anything for a few minutes.

And so began another tough stretch in our family's life—which became even tougher when, six weeks into my dad's radiation and chemo treatments, he was laid off from his sales job at Eaton Hydraulics, a diversified power management company. He was soon hired back with Eaton in another position, but he lost his company car and was forced to take a substantial pay cut. Fortunately, he was able to keep his health insurance.

In the following months, I began to see my dad's body deteriorate from not only the cancer but also the radiation and interferon treatments he was taking. He lost eighty-five pounds and slept about twenty hours a day. It was as if he had the flu for an entire year.

He really struggled, but I will never forget how he responded. He never lost his focus on being a father. In between his long naps, he came to all my games, still threw the baseball with me in the yard, still made sure I did my schoolwork, and still took me to church every Sunday. Nothing changed—nothing. As bad as I know he felt and as much as was on his mind, he was still the great dad he had always been. He never complained or questioned his sickness, even though he didn't know if he was going to live or not. I looked up to him for that. I still do.

Plus, he never lost his focus on God. I can remember nights when I'd get up at one or two in the morning and go to the kitchen for something to eat. Walking through the darkened living room, I'd turn on the light to see where I was going. My dad would often be on his knees, praying. That's an image that's burned in my mind forever.

Watching my dad and how he carried himself through his adversity helped me get through my ordeal with the Tuscaloosa tornado. Any time I felt a "poor me" coming on, I'd think back to my dad and what he had to face.

Of course, the financial part was weighing on him too. I could see that. Because of his pay cut, our family was really tight for money. So I decided to try expanding my summer lawn-mowing business as much as I could. That's when I first learned to promote and market something, just like I would later study in my classes at Alabama. I promoted my business throughout my church and to my teachers at school. I mowed some of the senior adults' yards, my teachers' yards, and my neighbors' yards. I cut grass all summer.

The only problem was, since I was just a kid, I needed a ride to most all my yards. But my dad was there for me every time. He would help me load up the lawn mower in the truck, take me there, then unload it so I could cut the grass. He was a huge help. I was never able to get that mower in and out of the truck by myself.

I worked hard and earned a good bit of money and gave the majority of it back to my parents. I don't know how much of a contribution it made, but I wanted to be a blessing to them.

My parents went through some very dark times while my dad was sick. That's why I wanted to help them. And it was so easy to give to them because they continued to invest generously in other people and give faithfully to the church. I liken it to the widow's mite story in the Bible, where the poor woman gave much more, percentage wise, than the rich people. That's exactly what my parents did.

Jesus talked about how, when you give, He makes sure you receive blessing in return. He said, "Give, and it will be given to you" (Luke 6:38). I saw this principle come true again and again. My parents would continue to give; they'd take some of my less fortunate friends out to dinner after church on Wednesdays; my dad would buy cleats for the guys on the team who couldn't afford any; and when my parents found themselves struggling, they would invariably find a check in the mail.

One of their friends sent a check one time with a letter saying, "God really just laid it on my heart that you could use this more than I could." This happened fairly often—which was crazy because my parents never told anyone about our financial situation. No one knew we could benefit from a little extra money, but people sent it anyway.

In the aftermath of the Tuscaloosa tornado, I certainly experienced many blessings through what so many people did for me. I saw firsthand how much it means when someone chooses to be a blessing to you. But the first place I learned it was from watching people come around us when I was just a kid and my parents were so sick. I never really told anyone how I felt about their illnesses, but somehow everybody who came or called knew exactly the right things to say.

Thankfully, Momma and Daddy both whipped cancer. It wasn't easy, but they made it through—through more than I could ever imagine. I know it made all of us stronger in our resolve and our attitudes.

Looking back, I appreciate them being so honest with me about their conditions. After both of them were completely well, they told me that during their illnesses, they didn't want to tell me they were going to die, but they also didn't want to tell me God was going to heal them or that they were going to be OK because they didn't want me mad at God if they didn't survive. They didn't want me to think God had let me down. They were careful, yet honest, about everything they told me. They prepared me for whatever the outcome might be.

My parents are the best.

———————

After my freshman year at Austin High School in Decatur, my dad, whose condition had improved, was offered an opportunity to return to a sales job with Eaton, covering a different territory of six or seven states throughout the Southeast. He was given the choice to move anywhere in Tennessee or Kentucky. So we packed our bags and moved to Murfreesboro, Tennessee.

I was excited about moving and seeing what else was out there. Murfreesboro is a rapidly growing town just outside of Nashville. The culture in Murfreesboro was so invigorating—small-town roots with a big-city vibe. It was a great experience living there.

And I think the change in scenery was good for us. It gave us sort of a new lease on life. Both of my parents were in remission from their cancers, so no one in Murfreesboro knew what we had gone through the previous few years. We believed God put us there to heal, recover, and be a family again.

I chose Riverdale High School to attend because of its excellent football program. The Warriors had won four state championships before I got there, produced college prospect athletes every year, were always ranked high in the preseason polls, and usually did a pretty good job in carrying out those predictions. When I got there, I was behind some talented players, but I really wanted to be able to contribute in any way I could.

Our coach at Riverdale was Ron Aydelott, a fine man and a heck of a football coach. He taught us so many things about life away from the football field. If there's one single thing I learned from him, it was something he'd always say to us: "Outwork the person who wants what you want."

That's been my mantra ever since—throughout football, school, the weight room, running, whatever. When I worked out in the weight room at Alabama, the linemen's platforms were right across from mine. I used them as examples; I always tried to out-lift them. I always wanted to be stronger than them and to outwork them. A lot of that drive came from Coach Aydelott.

One day during summer workouts before my first season as a sophomore, the coaches asked if any of us could long snap. I thought, *Hey, this is my chance.* From the time Coach Lindsey had taught me how to snap at Brookhaven Middle School, I had continued to practice it. My new coaches wanted proof, of course, so I asked them for a football, right there in the weight room, then snapped it to them. Just one time.

That's all they needed to see.

I won the job right there.

My sophomore year, all I worked on was long snapping. I only weighed about 185 pounds. I wasn't quite big enough to get much playing time on the offensive line. So for three hours a day, four days a week, for twenty weeks, I mastered the craft of long snapping while continuing to grow and get stronger. By the time I was a junior, I was up to about 215–220 pounds, able to contribute a little bit more on the offensive line as well, in addition to long snapping.

During that junior season, 2006, my dad took me to the Alabama-Ole Miss football game in Tuscaloosa. We walked around the Quad, watched the people tailgating, and soaked in the atmosphere. I remember telling my dad how bad I wanted this, how determined I was to play for a school like Alabama. Even today, I get chill bumps just thinking about that afternoon, telling him what I told him, and how things turned out from there.

In commemoration of Coach Paul "Bear" Bryant's historic 315th win twenty-five years earlier, the Alabama players wore special houndstooth-trimmed Nike jerseys for the game. Of course, Alabama never misses a beat, marketing-wise. I wanted one of those jerseys. So my dad bought one for me before the game at a souvenir stand.

Before the game, Daddy pointed out that Joe Namath was down on the Alabama sidelines. So I took my jersey down there to the fence and somehow got his attention. He came over and signed it for me. I felt like a million dollars. For me, it was just icing on the cake on a great day.

An unforgettable memory.

Little did I know, but just a few games later, Mike Shula would be out as Alabama's head coach. And in early 2007, when I heard Coach Nick Saban was coming to Alabama, I knew that's where I wanted to go. As I mentioned earlier, I had been an LSU baseball fan growing up, but when I started playing football in the fifth grade—the same time when Coach Saban was turning things around at LSU in football—I became a Saban fan too. I wasn't really an LSU football fan, but I really did like Coach Saban. I remember cheering him on when LSU won the national championship in 2003.

I knew if I was ever going to play anywhere at the next level, I needed to concentrate on my long snapping skills. That was my ticket. My difference. Several of my buddies at Riverdale went on to play college ball—David Sumrall, a tackle at Navy; Travis Lilienthal, a center at Middle Tennessee State; David Spurlock, a guard at Florida State, and Michael Pope, a guard at UT Martin. I was nowhere near their size. Nobody was going to pay any attention to me. So I just focused on snapping.

It's a little different now, but at the time I was coming out of high school, snappers were just about the last thing college coaches thought about during the recruiting process. So I knew that if I had any chance of playing at a big-time school, the best I could do was to be a walk-on. In order to get my name out, I went to the Chris Sailer Kicking/Rubio Long Snapping Camp in Las Vegas, as well as the Ray Guy/ Pro Kicker Camp in Bowling Green, Kentucky. One day while on the field at that camp, Ray Guy—a true kicking legend from his days with the Oakland Raiders—walked by and took note of my snapping. In making a point about something to a big group of guys, he asked me to snap to him. When I did, he said, "Great snap, son." I was on cloud nine after hearing that.

I also went to a number of special teams camps at different colleges around the country, which is pretty much equivalent to an open tryout in front of the coaches. I loved going to those camps. Snapping is fun for me; I truly enjoy it. I know that sounds crazy, and no one ever understands it, but there's an art to long snapping. We're a niche group.

I took those camps very seriously and really gave them my all. I was the MVP of the LSU camp, made the All-Saban team at the Alabama camp, and was ranked a five-star snapper and the No. 3 snapper in the country according to Chris Rubio on chrissailerkicking.com. I received scholarship offers from Washington State, Central Michigan, Eastern Michigan, and several smaller schools all over the country, but those places weren't where I wanted to play. I'm from the South, and I knew what a big deal Southeastern Conference football was. That's what I wanted to be doing on Saturdays in the fall.

I inquired with Alabama, of course, but the coaches told me they didn't really need any long snappers. This broke my heart because I knew I was good enough. I wanted to play there so bad to make my dad happy. Plus, I wanted to play for Coach Saban. My dad talked about how it would hurt him to cheer for other teams but that he would make himself do it . . . for me. He laughed, but I'm not so sure it wasn't killing him. I really wanted him to be able to say "Roll Tide" and cheer for his son all in the same breath.

But a lot of it wasn't up to me.

Coach Bradley Dale Peveto was at that time the special teams coach for LSU. He and I had a good relationship from his years as an assistant coach at Middle Tennessee State in Murfreesboro while I was playing high school ball there. I was asked to come to several games in Baton Rouge but was only able to attend one. Coincidentally, it was when they played Middle Tennessee. LSU won 44-0 and went on to win the national championship that year. I thought, with the Coach Peve connection, LSU might be the place for me. But

after the season he was named LSU's co-defensive coordinator, and Joe Robinson came from Arizona to replace him in
the special teams position. This put a halt to my recruiting
process at LSU. Coach Robinson, getting adjusted to his new
job, reached out to contact me a few times, but we never
talked in person, only back and forth over voicemails.

So heading into the final months of my senior year at
Riverdale, I had no idea where I was going to college. I knew
I was good enough to play at these schools, but I just couldn't
find the right fit.

It killed me. I was so stressed. My close friends had all
signed D-1 letters of intent months earlier, and I knew I was
as good as them. Why couldn't I find a school? Where was
I going to go?

Everybody comes to some of these moments in life. Big
decisions. Big unknowns. And at the height of the pressure
I was feeling, I decided to quit trying to force the situation,
stop worrying about it, and just pray about it—the old "let
go and let God" saying.

And about two weeks later, things started to happen.

Coach Bobby Williams, the special teams coach from
Alabama, called me. He explained how the backup snapper
they were counting on had torn his ACL, and he wanted to
know if I'd be able to come down for a visit and to watch a
spring scrimmage. I was all over it. I thought, *Finally, here's
an opportunity. That's all I want.*

My parents and I drove down to Tuscaloosa and watched
a Friday spring practice and Saturday scrimmage. I couldn't
have felt more welcomed down there. I was able to sit in on
meetings with the team, watch film, and tour the dorm and
academic facilities. I met all the coaches and was able to walk
around on the field at Bryant-Denny. My eyes were as big as
those fancy video boards in each corner. It was awesome.

I met with Coach Saban in his office and was able to experience the "remote control door" for the first time. When I sat down, he clicked a button on this remote, and all of a sudden the door to his office closed. I told him I had to get me one of those. I'm sure it was the millionth time he'd heard that, but he still got a chuckle from it.

Coach Saban talked briefly with my family and me about their situation at long snapper and what they planned on doing the next year. Then he went on to talk about the core values he instilled in his team—how discipline, commitment, leadership, and all the little things mattered. He made sure my family and I understood that if I came to Alabama, I was there first to get a college degree and that football would come second. My parents left there very impressed.

All I could think about was how awesome all of this was.

My future coach walked us to our car later that day and asked how everything went. I simply told him, "I want to play at Alabama. Where do I sign?"

CHAPTER 3

Ready for Some Football

In June 2008, shortly after high school graduation, I packed up all my clothes and stuff—including my fishing rod and tackle box—and headed down from Tennessee to Tuscaloosa in my truck. My mom rode with me, and Daddy followed behind us. I remember listening to the Eagles the entire time, which I would later learn is Coach Saban's all-time favorite group. My parents helped me move into Bryant Hall with my roommates Morgan Ogilvie, Dave Blalock, and Corey Smith. Later that day, I said good-bye and began my new life as a college student.

I was scared to death.

I had been working out for several weeks at the D1 Sports Training Center in Franklin, Tennessee, not far from home, so I *thought* I was in good shape. We ran and lifted every day, and they worked us pretty hard. I figured I'd be totally prepared when I got to Alabama.

Man, was I ever wrong.

I wasn't ready at all for Coach Scott Cochran and his summer workouts. Frankly, there's *nothing* I could have done to get ready for them. Coach Cochran knows exactly how much you can take. He doesn't give you more than you can bear at any one time, but he sure is tough. There's always a reason for it—it's meant to make you better—but *grueling* doesn't even come close to describing it. I know one thing: it was the first time I'd ever thrown up from running.

My older teammates took me under their wing that summer and helped me get through the initial growing pains. In later years, whenever I'd see a new guy struggling, I always tried to emulate the encouragement I'd received as a freshman, because I understood how tough it was. That's why football creates such a brotherhood between teammates.

Working out with Coach Cochran and his staff got my body in excellent physical shape. And mentally, the *PX2* classes prepared our minds for what being an Alabama football player really means.

I've always been a very motivated, driven person, but the *PX2* classes helped me pinpoint my mental weaknesses and develop my strengths. *PX2* is a program put together by the Pacific Institute that teaches goal setting and how to develop self-confidence, self-esteem, and ethical behavior. It's just one example of the great learning opportunities Coach Saban brings to his football program.

One of the biggest things I learned in *PX2* was "self-talk"—that we're always telling ourselves something, whether we're aware of it or not. We're either telling ourselves we can or we can't. This can be used in any facet of life.

For instance, if I'm outside running 110s in 100-degree weather, and I'm telling myself how hot it is and how much I'm hurting, then I've already beaten myself. But if I constantly repeat in my head, *I've got this; I've put in the time; I've put in the effort, I'll finish the job,* then I'll accomplish what I've set out to do. Our minds are our strongest muscle. Our thoughts lead directly to actions. What we tell ourselves has a direct link to what we do.

What are you telling yourself today?

Gaining this kind of knowledge during that first summer gave me an edge on the football field. I then started applying all these things to the classroom and other areas of my life. I didn't come to school just to sign a roll; I came to school to compete, to get better—in sports and in everything. My entire attitude about school changed when I started looking at it this way.

Being able to watch Coach Saban and his staff and how they work every day was a great learning experience for me. Day in, day out, these guys dedicate themselves to be the best, and they help every member of their team be the best—the best player, the best student, the best person. Everything after that will take care of itself.

The first time I heard Coach Saban speak to the team, I could feel the motivation firing up inside me. "We're not going to focus on winning championships," he said. "We're going to focus on building a team full of champions, and then the championships will come." Coach is always talking about buying into the team. And as soon as he said that, I was all in.

My first season in 2008, I made the squad of 105 and was able to go to camp in early August. I know it's called "practice" in college and "camp" in the pros, but during that grueling two and a half weeks between reporting day and the day classes start, it's definitely CAMP. We ate, slept, and breathed football.

Going into the season, Coach Saban told us we had everything it took to be a good team—a good offense, a good quarterback, a good defense, and good specialists. But, of course, you don't really know what kind of team you've got until you buckle your chinstraps and play a game.

It didn't take but one game for us to find out. Playing in the Georgia Dome, we soundly whipped No. 9 Clemson, 34–10. Even though I was being redshirted, my coaches let me travel and dress for the games as a reward for all my hard work.

I'll never forget that experience—the flight from Tuscaloosa to Atlanta, staying at the Omni Hotel downtown, the tons of Alabama fans everywhere, running out of the tunnel alongside my fellow specialists, the resounding roars of "Roll Tide" shaking the roof of the Georgia Dome, and then dominating the Tigers from start to finish.

And when I say dominate, I mean it. A couple of freshmen named Julio Jones and Mark Ingram made their Crimson Tide debuts in the win. John Parker Wilson had a solid game at quarterback and our defense played lights-out. After that game, we realized we were legitimate—as good as Coach Saban said we could be. We really believed in ourselves for the first time.

I mention Julio and Mark, but looking back at that 2008 recruiting class, I think it'll go down as one of the greatest in Alabama football history, maybe the best ever. Besides those two, we had Mark Barron, Courtney Upshaw, Terrence Cody (a junior college transfer), Barrett Jones, Jerrell Harris, Dont'a Hightower, Michael Williams, Brad Smelley, Damion Square, and Marcell Dareus. In that group alone, eight went on to make first-team All-American. And for me—a walk-on long snapper—to be in the same class as those guys was, well, quite an honor.

After a surprisingly easy win at Arkansas in week four, our next big test was against Georgia in Athens in what they called the "Blackout" game, where their players and fans all wore black. Georgia was ranked No. 3, and everybody was talking about how good they were, how they were going to contend for the national championship. Coach Mark Richt had finally, supposedly, put together everything he needed to win it all.

I know why they do those blackout, whiteout things. Gets the fans all worked up. Creates a lot of energy and buzz in the stadium. But Coach Saban always shot down whatever effect those hyped-up marketing gimmicks were supposed to inflict on us before we ever took the field. He told us a story about his Michigan State team going into South Bend and whipping Notre Dame in one of the Irish's "Greenout" games, right there in front of "Touchdown Jesus" and everybody. The outcome of the Georgia game, he told us, would be determined by what we did, not what their fans were doing or what color jerseys their players were wearing. It's obvious, I know, but players need to hear that.

We took his message to heart. By halftime, we were up 31–0, and though Georgia came back within two touchdowns early in the second half—31–17—we pulled away from there. A few late fourth-quarter points made the final score sound close at 41–30, but losing was never a threat down the stretch. That was one of my all-time favorite Alabama games. And we dominated. After that one, everybody knew we were a force to be reckoned with, not only in the SEC but throughout the country.

As the season progressed, we picked up a lot of steam and momentum. Players who hadn't fully bought into what Coach Saban had been talking about at first began to see that it worked. It got to the point where no one questioned him—everybody just did what he said.

We went on to win every game of the regular season, including shutting out Auburn 36–0 after having lost to them the previous six years. Going from a 6–6 regular season mark the year before to 12–0 was quite a feat, but it was a direct result of our guys believing in Coach Saban.

So our goal to play in the SEC Championship Game in Atlanta became a reality. After the win over Auburn, we were undefeated and ranked No. 1. Our opponent was Florida, which was 11–1 and ranked No. 2. At stake was not only the SEC championship but a berth in the BCS National Championship Game.

Despite our third-quarter lead, Florida came back to beat us behind the late-game heroics of quarterback Tim Tebow and then went on to win the BCS title over Oklahoma. The Florida game was sure disappointing—as was the loss to Utah in the Sugar Bowl—but several good, positive things came out of them.

After the season, everyone committed to themselves and to the team this wasn't going to happen the next year.

And sure enough, it didn't.

Just two words make all the difference: National Championship.

Of course, all players come to Alabama knowing about its rich football history, the national titles, the All-Americans, the tradition, and so forth. It's kinda hard to get around in Tuscaloosa without seeing or hearing something about it. Just take a peek into Rama Jama's across the street from the stadium, where owner Gary Lewis displays about as much

Crimson Tide memorabilia as the Bryant Museum, not to mention cooking up the best breakfast in town.

I know Alabama fans—especially the older ones—have experienced multiple national championships. They have their special stories to tell. When I see such folks in places like Rama Jama's, it's a thrill for me to see the gleam in their eyes talking about Coach Bryant's first title in 1961, or the Goal Line Stand following the 1978 season, or Coach Stallings' march to the championship in 1992. Alabama fans take ownership in whatever happens on the field, good and bad. And frankly, we wouldn't want it any other way.

But as a player, until you hoist that trophy yourself, or feel the crimson and white confetti rain down on your head, or get sized for that national championship ring, you just can't realize how big it really is.

In 2009, we found out.

Beginning with a ten-point win over No. 7 Virginia Tech in the Chick-fil-A Kickoff Game in the Georgia Dome, and ending with the dismantling of Texas in the BCS National Championship Game, it was indeed a storybook season.

As much as I'd like to say I had a big role in those games, I can't. As a second-year freshman, I played behind senior long snapper Brian Selman, a guy who taught me so much and who remains a great friend today. But as Coach Saban often says, *everybody* on the team contributes, whether you play in a game or not. Every workout, every practice, every film study, every running session—we all play an important role in the success of our team. Although we might not get much (or any) playing time, we're there to be encouragers and to always be ready if we're asked to step in.

Our opener against Virginia Tech may have had more to do with establishing an identity and setting the tone of our season than any game we played. Despite dominating the game statistically, we were behind 17–16 going into the fourth quarter. And with Virginia Tech's talent, particularly on special teams, we just never knew what could happen.

There's a reason our players and fans hold up four fingers going into the final quarter, a tradition among Tide fans that I believe started back in the 1960s with Coach Bryant's teams. This symbolic gesture says the "Fourth Quarter's Ours." It says that despite what's happened up to then, or regardless of the score, we're going to dominate the fourth quarter. That's why our off-season workout regimen is called the "Fourth Quarter Program." It challenges us to reach down and gather up every ounce of determination to win, especially during the home stretch of a game. It's a mind-set of finishing what you started.

The fourth quarter of that game did indeed become ours, as Mark Ingram scored two touchdowns and Leigh Tiffin added a field goal in our 34–24 win. In the end, Leigh scored 14 of our 34 points (four field goals and two extra points), a great way to start what would become an All-American year for him.

Also in that game, Brian recovered a fumble on a punt return—leading to one of Leigh's field goals—so we "specialists" were really excited after that game, especially since Virginia Tech was so well known for their special teams play. Leigh's 14 points and Brian's fumble recovery were just affirmations of how special our special teams really were.

I'll be honest—we didn't play our best in a few games that season. Several times we faced adversity and had our backs against the wall, but we kept fighting. Games against Ole Miss and South Carolina, for example, were fairly close by our standards. And then there was the unforgettable

Tennessee game, when Terrence Cody blocked the potential game-winning field goal on the last play. That was one of those "whew" games, when you know you're the better team but things just don't go right. The crazy postgame celebration on the field that afternoon was one that'll never be topped.

No, wait—maybe this did. For me. After big wins over LSU and Mississippi State, my dream of actually playing in a game for the Crimson Tide finally came true. In the second half against Chattanooga on November 21, I got to snap for two field goals and an extra point.

I can't describe how pumped I was.

From the day in 2006 when my dad took me to campus for the Alabama-Ole Miss game—the day I really fell in love with the place—I had dreamed of getting on that turf and playing where so many legends had played. Although I had put in my time on the practice fields and on the sidelines, there was nothing quite like *being there*.

What a moment.

Then there was the Auburn game in Auburn—last game of the season, of course—another one in which we didn't play well. Despite falling behind early, catching up, and then trailing almost the entire fourth quarter, we pulled it out 26–21 with about a minute to go. On our winning drive, I stood on the sidelines in amazement watching Greg McElroy and Julio Jones hook up for completion after completion, four of which were for critical first downs.

The game-winning pass from Greg to Roy Upchurch was much more than just the decisive touchdown. It was icing on the cake for Roy after an up-and-down, injury-riddled career. Roy was one of those guys who, at first, didn't fully buy in to Coach Saban's discipline. Finally, though, as a senior, he understood what it took to be a winner and the sacrifices that had to be made. It was poetic justice that Roy would score the winning touchdown over Auburn to keep our national championship hopes alive. What an immensely talented player.

Before we could even think about playing for a national championship, however, we first needed to win the Southeastern Conference. As exciting as our season had been, our 12–0 record meant nothing. We hadn't won anything, other than the SEC Western Division title. We needed a win in the conference championship to get what we'd really come for: the BCS National Championship Game.

And standing in our way—again—were the top-ranked Florida Gators.

Many have said it's easier to win the national title than the SEC title, and I agree. Once a battle-tested SEC champion gets to the national championship game, history tells you the chances are good they're going to win. But as odd as this may sound, we weren't really worried about Florida. No disrespect to them, but we were concerned only with ourselves. We knew if we did what we needed to do as a team and everybody did his job as a player, we would come out on top that day. We all had such a peace about that game. You could feel it.

So our 32–13 win was certainly no surprise to us. Without a doubt, it was the best game we'd played all year, maybe one of the best in Alabama football history in terms of importance and performance. Afterward, we knew we had a very special team.

And a week later, we even had a very special Heisman Trophy winner. Words can't describe how thrilled we were to see Mark Ingram bring home Alabama's first Heisman. I know it seems like there should have been a half dozen or more Heisman winners from Alabama throughout history, but no—Mark was the first in 2009. During his acceptance speech, when he started crying, so did I. And I know I wasn't the only one. Several teammates told me they did too.

Mark talked about it being a team award, and he gave credit to his teammates, especially his offensive line. He went on to thank so many other people—his coaches, the trainers, the interns, the strength staff, the sports information guys, University President Robert Witt, Athletics Director Mal Moore, and even his teachers.

I was so proud of Mark. I felt like I was up there with him accepting that award. We all did. Here's someone I had worked out with every day, run beside in 100-degree weather, and lifted weights with. Granted, he did a lot more on the field than me, but that was fine. I'm honored to call Mark a teammate and a friend. And a Heisman Trophy winner.

———

With an SEC championship under our belts, it was off to Pasadena and the Rose Bowl for the BCS game. I've mentioned a few times about Alabama's tradition and all, but to be honest we didn't really know much about Alabama's Rose Bowl history, other than that line from the fight song: "Remember the Rose Bowl, we'll win then."

Believe me, after winning that game, we know all about it now.

To get us away from the hustle and bustle, the bowl arranged for us to stay in Costa Mesa, about an hour southeast of Los Angeles. Other than going to a huge mall across the street, there really wasn't much to do there, but we actually welcomed the relaxed atmosphere. The year before, it was obvious by the way we played in the Sugar Bowl that New Orleans was too big a distraction for us.

In order to keep both teams from having to deal with potential traffic problems getting to the stadium on game day, we were relocated to Pasadena the night before. For our team movie that evening, we watched *Miracle*, the story of the 1980 U.S. Olympic hockey team's emotional victory over Russia in the semifinal game. The parallels to our situation were obvious: our win in the SEC Championship Game against Florida would mean very little if we didn't beat Texas. Just like our Olympic hockey team, we still had a game to play. For them, it was Finland for the gold medal. For us, it was Texas for the BCS National Championship.

In the locker room before the game, Coach Saban talked about how hard we had worked all year to create an identity for how we play, of our physicality and our mental edge. He said if we continued this identity, we'd be national champions. It was our time, and if we played our best, we would not be denied. And sure enough, everything he said came true.

I have many great memories of that game—especially our big plays—but for me the pregame ceremony really sticks out. Running out of that tunnel into the famed Rose Bowl Stadium and seeing all the people and those thousands of camera flashes was a humbling and thrilling experience.

Josh Groban sang the National Anthem, accompanied on bass guitar by Flea from the Red Hot Chili Peppers. As Groban sang the words, "And the rockets' red glare, the bombs bursting in air," a barrage of fireworks went off behind the stage. Then after they finished, more fireworks lit up the sky. As Flea was walking off the field toward our sideline, he looked at Brian Selman and me square in the eyes and said, "Roll Tide!" We got a kick out of that.

As if those fireworks weren't enough, more exploded outside the stadium right before the coin toss, all of which resulted in a haze of smoke that lingered over the field the entire game. From then on, every time we watched any film from that game, the smoke would be there, even into the fourth quarter.

Although Texas made it interesting late, we went on to win, 37–21. When Eryk Anders sacked the Texas quarterback and Courtney Upshaw recovered the fumble on the 2-yard line to seal the outcome, I was standing right next to Morgan Ogilvie, and we looked at each other and said—at the same exact time—"We're going to win the national championship!"

Our locker room after the game was crazy, like a huge party. Everybody was hugging each other, taking photos and videos, yelling and screaming. And when we sang the fight song and got to that verse, "Remember the Rose Bowl, we'll win then," we screamed it at the top of our lungs. Singing those words after such a historic win is something that'll stick with me forever.

It's hard to believe, but the seventeen years between Alabama's 1992 and 2009 national championships was the second longest gap between titles in school history. As a team, we were honored to get the Alabama program back on track, just like the old days.

———————

As excited as we were, after winning it all in 2009, we were equally as disappointed about our 10–3 season in 2010.

Looking back, I wonder how a team so talented, deep, and athletic could lose three games. Granted, we'd lost nine defensive starters from our championship team, including great players such as Javier Arenas, Terrence Cody, Rolando McClain, and Kareem Jackson. But we felt good about the guys coming back like Marcell Dareus, Mark Barron, Dont'a Hightower, Dre Kirkpatrick, Dee Milliner, Robert Lester, C. J. Mosley, and the young depth behind them. With Barrett Jones and James Carpenter anchoring the offensive line, Greg McElroy under center, Julio Jones catching everything in sight, and the one-two punch of Mark Ingram and Trent Richardson in the backfield, we didn't see anyone being able to stop us.

Except, of course, ourselves.

And we just never saw that coming.

As talented as we were, we just didn't have the right mind-set or the right leadership in 2010. Coach Saban warned us repeatedly that our team was not the 2009 team, that we had a new schedule, many new faces, and—as expected—a target on our back. As much as the national media likes to make you think the defending national champions show up the next year with the same exact team, it just doesn't happen that way. Every year has its differences. No two are exactly the same.

In Dr. Ron Dulek's GBA 490 business class at Alabama, we learned about the Icarus Factor, when companies or organizations put tons of energy and ambition into a new project, only to watch it fail. They don't realize while it's happening that their project is being fueled totally on excitement, not on the foundational principles required for success. They were so focused on winning, they forgot to focus on the process.

That's a succinct, nutshell way to describe our 2010 team. Lots of hype, talent galore, defending national champions, high expectations. But our focus the entire season was on winning—that's all—without taking the steps necessary to make us win. The game against South Carolina was a good example: we played poorly, didn't have the right attitude, and ran up against a team determined to beat us. Later losses to LSU (by three points) and Auburn (by one point) were just continuations of that same poor mind-set.

To get a snapshot of just how talented our 2010 team was, look at the final score of the Capital One Bowl: Alabama 49, Michigan State 7. That game was much more indicative of our team's talent than our 10–3 record showed.

Personally, this season was a memorable one for me, since it was my first year to start as our long snapper. Leading up to the season, I was dedicated to getting in shape, eating right, and doing all the things necessary to be a champion. In both our Fourth Quarter Program in the winter and the summer workout program, I won the team competition (sixteen 110s, ten 40s, and bench press) based on points awarded by position, expectations, and goals. In every workout, I couldn't help but think back to my parents and what they went through during their bouts with cancer. I'd say to myself, over and over, *If my parents can do what they did, then I can do this to the best of my ability, no matter how hot it is or how I feel.* That's a mind-set I'll carry with me the rest of my life. It's certainly the mind-set I carried throughout that solid but frustrating season.

I'll say this much, however, about our bowl game win: it was more than just a 49–7 blowout. It was a confidence-builder, a shot in the arm, an optimistic sign of things to come. Just as we used losses to Florida and Utah in 2008 to motivate us toward the national title run in 2009, we used our bowl win as a springboard to bigger and better things the next season.

And we wasted no time in doing it.

The very next day—literally—after returning from Orlando, we were back at it: lifting, running, and getting better. That's just the way they do it around there.

But as much preparation and planning as we did for the 2011 season, nothing would prepare us or me for what would transpire in slightly less than five months' time.

Nothing could've prepared us for that.

CHAPTER 4

Life on 25th Street

I loved my little house at 611 25th Street in Tuscaloosa.

Located in the heart of town, just five minutes from campus and less than two miles from the football practice field, it was a dream house for a college kid like me. Four bedrooms, about fifteen hundred square feet, a huge back-yard, the massive field across the street, and great neighbors. And the rent was cheap.

How we found it was by random chance. After living in Bryant Hall during the 2008–2009 school year, I shared a condominium with a friend in the summer and fall of 2009. But condo living was not for me. I wanted to round up a couple of roommates and get a house.

One of my friends, Alan Estis, who had lived next to me in Bryant Hall, and Ryan Henley, a football manager, said they'd go in with me on a house if we could find a good deal. Alan's mom found a realtor with several houses for rent, including the one on 25th Street. We went out, looked at it, and loved it. It was the third house from the end of a dead-end street.

We moved into it in early 2010, the spring semester of my sophomore season. And somehow, some way, we kept three guys in there the whole time. We had kind of a revolving door—one would move out and another would move in. As long as the rent was paid, we didn't care. Even my friend Leigh Tiffin, our All-American kicker, stayed with us for about five months when he was in town training for the NFL Combine.

On its own, the house was a perfect place to live, no matter the location. But throw in the field across the street, and the place became magical. Right there in the geographical center of Tuscaloosa, just blocks away from the hustle and bustle of campus and Tuscaloosa's busiest thoroughfares, was this peaceful and serene patch of green, filled with beautiful oaks, pecan trees, walnut trees, and pastureland.

Nestled between our street on the south, the Glendale Gardens neighborhood on the west, and the Hillcrest neighborhood on the north, this oasis served as my getaway spot, my safe haven. Whatever distractions or baggage were hanging around in my life never went to the field with me. Every time I headed that way to hit golf balls or play with our dogs, I checked my worries and frustrations at the gate. I guess we all need a place like that.

Having cut a lot of grass as a teenager and knowing what a tough job it is, I never took for granted someone's toil in keeping this field so pristine. It was as if they kept it cut just for me. I did my best to take care of the field and keep it clean and picked up. But I always wondered how such a prime piece of property had managed to stay undeveloped.

Then one day, I met Jim and Mary Jean Johnson, who live in one of the big houses in the Hillcrest neighborhood on the north end of the field. From the Johnsons I learned that back in the 1930s, three University of Alabama professors purchased around forty acres from the University, which had owned the land since the 1800s. Each of the professors carved out six acres for themselves, then subdivided the remainder into what's now Hillcrest. In the 1970s, the Johnsons purchased a home on one of the six-acre tracts and, along with their next-door neighbors the Prices (also owners of a six-acre tract), assumed responsibility for maintaining the field.

Not a day went by that I didn't stand on my front porch and marvel at this beautiful setting. Lining the fences behind the Glendale Gardens homes were crepe myrtles as far as I could see. Dogwoods and loropetalum lit up the sky in springtime like a fireworks show. Ivy-covered stone walls, picket fences, beautiful flowers, fountains, bees making honey, and even a greenhouse were within easy sight. Every home owner in Glendale Gardens really knew how to keep up a backyard.

But living at our house meant so much more to me than the great location, the scenery, the cheap rent, or even serving as my place of refuge. You just never know who God might put in your path or in whose path He might put you. One thing I know for certain—if I hadn't been living at 611 25th Street, I probably never would have met Ashley Harrison.

One night in the summer of 2010, my friend Trent was having a little get-together a few houses down the street and invited me over to hang out. As I mentioned earlier, I was focused on getting in the best shape I could for the season—my first year to start as the Tide's long snapper—and all I had on my mind was football.

While I was chatting with some folks, Trent came over and said, "Hey, man, come here. I want you to meet my sister."

I thought, *Trent's sister? Trent doesn't have a sister.*

Seeing as how Trent was just a crazy, messy college kid, I didn't know what to imagine this girl could be like, whoever she really was. But then we walked up to this beautiful brunette wearing a purple tank top and blue jeans, and Trent said to her, "Hey, Punk, meet my buddy Carson I've been telling you about."

This girl shook my hand and said, "Hey, Carson, my name's Ashley," looking me in the eye with a smile that was just so genuine. Then after a quick "nice to meet you," she went back to chatting with her friends.

I just stood there, watched her for a moment, then looked at Trent and said, "We have to do something about your 'sister.' She's gorgeous."

As the night went on, I told myself I was going to get to know Ashley. I started walking around the house looking for her. When I finally found her, she was sitting on the couch. She looked at me as if she knew I had been looking for her. She seemed to know I thought she was beautiful and that I wanted to find out more about her.

Standing up, she grabbed my hand, and said, "Let's go sit on the back porch."

I don't remember anything we said to each other after that. All I remember is laughing—laughing harder than I'd laughed in a long time. I would crack jokes on her, and instead of getting her feelings hurt, she would crack jokes right back at me, and we'd just laugh and laugh, the same thing I do with all of my friends. Although we were together only a few hours that night, I felt like I had known Ashley for a long time. I felt comfortable around her. I was just able to be myself, and we had so much fun.

Ashley and I continued to hang out together the next couple of weeks—just friends having fun. Then one day we were watching TV, and I stepped out on a limb, asking if she'd be my girlfriend. I was so nervous asking her, but I had to. This girl was awesome. I was crazy about her.

She looked at me, laughed, and said, "Of course I will, Carson." I don't know what she saw in me, but I'm glad she saw it.

Ashley was from Dallas. I never could tell if she had city roots or country roots because she was the perfect mix of both. Her parents obviously raised her well. She went to Ursuline Academy, where she made a perfect 36 on her ACT and played lacrosse and volleyball. Her mother, Darlene, is one of the most successful realtors in Dallas, and Ashley grew up wanting to be a successful businesswoman like her mom. She wanted to go to a college that had good academics but still had a good college atmosphere, including sorority life, a small-town feel, and, of course—football. What better place than Alabama?

Ashley came to college on a full academic scholarship and majored in economics, one of the hardest majors by far. One time I saw her in the library with a roomful of math and finance whizzes, and I felt bad for her because I thought she must be struggling in a class or something. Walking over to their table, though, I found she was teaching all of them how to do some of the more difficult problems. My friend and teammate Morgan Ogilvie, who is one of the smartest guys I know, would always ask me if it was OK for him to study with Ashley because she knew more about the subject than anyone. She was set to graduate in May 2011 and was planning on going to law school. With a 4.13 GPA and a 168 on her LSAT, she wouldn't have any trouble going anywhere she wanted.

Pretty obvious, then, I got the best end of this deal. When I met her, I was just some country dirt leg from Tennessee, thinking about nothing else but football and getting ready for the upcoming season. She was this smart, sophisticated young woman focused on school and her future. I had a lot to learn from her.

We dated for almost a year, and I will never forget the impact she had on my life. I wanted to be like her. The passion she had for life was incredible. We would talk about what we wanted to do after college and our futures, and she made me feel like I could do anything. She would push me in everything, and I loved it. No matter how small or pointless any of my accomplishments were, she would always tell me how proud she was of me. And I knew she meant it.

Ashley wasn't like a lot of girls. She was completely different. I remember when we first started dating, she went and got her nails done trying to impress me. She came over to my house all dressed up, and my roommates and I were across the street in the field throwing baseball. Ashley walked out there, and I started thinking, *Aw, man, I guess it's time to go in.* But she just put that freshly French manicured hand in that old leather baseball glove and played catch with us. I would throw the baseball to her as hard as I could, and she would catch it with no problem, then throw it right back to me.

When Ashley set her schedule for the fall, she needed to take a class I was already enrolled in, so she registered for the same one. Needless to say, I made an A, not because I cheated but because she made me study with her. I was amazed watching her work, not only the way she could soak it all in but how she could teach it to others. She was so disciplined and focused on the task at hand.

One day we were sitting in this class and saw an ad in *The Crimson White* student newspaper for a black Labrador retriever. She showed it to me and said, "We're going to go get it. Right now." Ashley thought Josey (my German shepherd named after Josey Wales from my favorite Clint Eastwood movie) needed a friend. So we slipped out of class and went to pick up this gorgeous purebred black Lab puppy that carried a stud pedigree. I'm sure there was some duck hunter somewhere so mad that Ashley and I had found this dog because she was a natural. We didn't train her to do what she did; she was born to do it.

Ashley wanted to name her all these crazy names I would've been embarrassed to call the dog in public. We finally said her name would be Bottega, after some designer Ashley really liked, but we would just call her B. It took us three days to decide on a name, yet it took B only one day to learn it. The dog was brilliant. B and Josey were like sisters. They played all day, all the time.

Right by my front door, I kept a pitching wedge and several golf balls. As soon as I touched that club, Josey would run wild, jumping and running around in circles like it was the greatest day of her life. B was still learning, but she got excited because Josey was excited. So I'd get that club and those balls, and we'd go across the street, walk through the gate, and forget about whatever was behind us.

I guess Josey and B left their dog cares behind, too, because when we got out there, they'd go crazy. I'd hit a wedge shot and they'd race to retrieve it. They would even fight over which one could get there first and bring the ball back to me. All I did was hit; they would do the rest. I always wondered what kind of chaos we would've caused if I'd ever taken them to a real golf course. If there's such a thing as dog heaven, that was it. I was honored to be a part of their fun and frolicking.

The serenity of life at 611 25th Street was good, at least until Wednesday, April 27, 2011. That's the day when, in less than a minute, all our fun and frolicking went away.

CHAPTER 5

Aftershock

"... ley!"

That second syllable of Ashley's name, shouted at the top of my lungs, is the first thing I remember after the tornado ripped us out of the house. Screaming her name was what jarred me conscious enough to realize that something terrible had happened and that Ashley was nowhere to be found. It was all a blur, a moment in time when I wondered if I was in some horrific dream.

I remember very little about the few hours following the tornado, but with help from several others, I now have a good idea of what transpired.

Within a few minutes after our house was destroyed, Alan, who for the most part was uninjured, found me face-down in what was left of the field across the street. At first, he thought I was dead. He rolled me over, shook me, and said, "Carson! Carson!" and I came to. I don't remember any of that, nor do I remember Alan even being there. All I recall is standing up right after that and yelling for Ashley.

I remember looking around and asking myself, *All right, what just happened?* I couldn't really process that a tornado had come through, but I knew I was standing in the middle of a catastrophe. My place of solitude, where I would romp with Josey and B and leave all my cares behind, was torn to pieces. The massive oaks and pecan trees were ripped out of the ground or snapped in two. Remnants of whole houses cluttered the ground. The beautiful Glendale Gardens neighborhood was but a shell of itself. All those nice fences and gardens and crepe myrtles and fountains had been wiped away.

I said to myself, *OK, the tornado happened after all. Now I've got to get everybody together. People are counting on me. People's moms are counting on me.* I remember standing there and thinking, *OK, Carson, get your act together.*

I saw Payton crawling in the street, heading my way. He finally stood to his feet, limping badly. When he reached me, he handed me his phone and said, "Here, talk to my mom."

I said, "Hello?"

Payton's mom said, "Carson, what happened?" Payton was in so much shock, he hadn't known what to tell her.

"We're fine," I told her, "we're not hurt. We're just trying to find Ashley. We'll call you back."

Using Payton's phone, I called my mom and told her the same thing—that we were fine and were trying to find Ashley. It's a miracle I even remembered her phone number. She said she and my dad would get to Tuscaloosa as soon as possible from Birmingham. (My parents had moved from Murfreesboro to Birmingham in 2009.)

What my and Payton's moms gathered from our brief end of the conversation and what had actually happened were two entirely different things. Based on what I told my mom, she assumed we were fine and not injured, that the tornado had not hit our house, and that Ashley was only temporarily out of pocket, possibly at work.

The truth, of course, was that our house had just been picked up and thrown across the street. With us *in* it. Payton was in shock and could barely walk; I was in shock, concussed, delirious, and torn up from head to toe; and Ashley, who had been with us in the closet just a minute or two before . . .

Ashley was missing.

Continuing our search, we headed back toward where our house once stood and did a huge loop around our street for a few minutes. I can't begin to explain how dangerous this was, especially with us in our condition, debris on the ground, power lines down all over the streets, and gas leaks everywhere. The whole place could have blown up in a second.

As we were frantically yelling for Ashley, our neighbors Clay and Juli Carter, who lived three houses down, ran to us. They had ridden out the storm in their bathtub and were not hurt. Taking one look at us, they knew we needed immediate assistance. So, helping us to their driveway, they sat us down in some chairs, got us some water, ice, and blankets, and tended to our wounds with rubbing alcohol. From all accounts, we stayed there for about forty-five minutes.

I can't imagine how crazy and goofy we all sounded. We had just gone through the worst few seconds of our lives, and it was nearly impossible to soak it all in. One minute we're crammed in a closet riding out a tornado, and several minutes later we're sitting campfire-style in our neighbor's driveway, in shock, wrapped in blankets, cut up all over, having absolutely no idea the magnitude of what just happened.

Clay and Juli say I kept asking the same four questions the whole time, over and over:

"Where's Ashley?"

"Where are the dogs?"

"Where are my parents? I need to talk to my parents." (I didn't remember I had already talked to my mom.)

"Is this over?" (The tornado, I guess.)

And unknowingly, adding a lighthearted moment to the situation, I also asked several times out loud, "Why am I wearing a bathing suit?" When I wasn't asking questions, they tell me I was repeating the same four words: "We gotta find Ashley, we gotta find Ashley, we gotta find Ashley."

While caring for us, Juli was having some kind of a panic attack herself, and she said I kept telling her, "Juli, you've gotta get your act together because we need help. You have to help us. We need you right now. And we gotta find Ashley. We gotta find Ashley."

While Clay stayed with us, Juli went looking for Bob White, a Tuscaloosa police officer who lived nearby. While she was gone, some guy in a flak jacket was running around doing triage. He wrapped my wrist up in a chamois cloth, kind of like a medical paper towel. I remember thanking him. He said, "You're welcome," then he took off to find someone else. I thought, *That guy is a hero. He's going to save someone's life tonight.*

Juli came back soon after that and said, "Bob has made arrangements to get you to the hospital. Let's go." Alan stayed with Clay at the house while Payton and I hobbled up the street a couple of blocks to a police car. For Payton and me, it was a real struggle to get there. My ankle was badly hurt, while Payton had what would later be diagnosed as a strained posterior cruciate knee ligament. But with all the streets blocked by downed trees and power lines, we had no other choice but to walk.

When we finally reached the police cruiser, Payton couldn't bend his hurt knee, so he had to practically lie down in the backseat. We were taken to an awaiting ambulance, then it was off to DCH Regional Medical Center.

The whole way there, I couldn't help but wonder, *Where is Ashley?*

CHAPTER 6

Answers

DCH, especially its Emergency Room, was an absolute train wreck.

At least that's what I'm told today because my memory of it is a fuzzy, clouded mess.

They say for about thirteen hours, from the time the tornado roared through Tuscaloosa a little after 5:00 p.m. until daybreak the next morning, about nine hundred folks were processed and treated there. Some of them walked in with minor injuries. Others were brought in unconscious on homemade plywood stretchers. They came by foot, by ambulance, by car, by police cruiser, and—when the weather cleared—by helicopter. Age, color, wealth, or social status made no difference. This violent twister touched down into all walks of Tuscaloosa life.

Imagine hundreds of people trying to fit into a space designed for only a few handfuls. Every possible square inch of DCH was used as a treatment and triage area—the auditorium, the cath lab, the outpatient surgery areas, the hallways, even the cafeteria. Kids searched for their parents. Parents desperately sought their children.

I later read where one of the doctors on duty described the scene as a "war zone," with the power knocked out and people everywhere. Doctors and nurses from all over Tuscaloosa—including retirees from years before—descended upon the hospital to offer assistance. There's no telling how many lives were saved by these heroes of the medical community. What a blessing they were to Tuscaloosa that day.

When I finally got there myself, they strapped me to a board for stability. I guess that's standard protocol for concussion patients or anyone with suspected neck or back injuries. And for the longest time after I arrived, I just lay in a hallway, staring at the ceiling. I had a concussion and was probably still in shock, so I was completely out of it. I was still worried about Ashley, but at the same time I was delusional. I couldn't process what was going on, and on a couple of occasions I couldn't even remember where I was.

Looking around at one point, I saw Dr. Jimmy Robinson, one of our Alabama team doctors. I yelled, "Hey, Dr. Rob, what's up, man?" He looked at me, like, *Oh my gosh, this is one of our players!* He was treating all kinds of people he didn't know; yet I was someone he was accustomed to seeing three or four times a week. He was quite surprised to see me there.

As crazy as the ER was, the hospital personnel did a great job tending to all of us. I remember a nurse named Mandy who kept checking on me. I didn't want her to leave my side—not that I really needed anything—but because I had absolutely no idea what was going on. She did a great job of keeping me settled down while coaching the student nurses on what to do.

Around 9:00, my parents arrived, which was a miracle in itself. When they had left Birmingham around 5:30—just minutes after I had talked to my mom on the phone—the tornado, having already ripped through Tuscaloosa, Alberta

City, and Holt, was now headed their way. Having no idea where it might go, they just took off on a whim and a prayer, trusting the Lord they would make it safely. My mom says they reached Tuscaloosa in about thirty minutes. I'm afraid to do the math on how fast they drove.

Unaware that I had been taken to the hospital, Momma and Daddy headed toward my neighborhood, but the closest they could get was about a mile away. After parking in the Zap Photography parking lot on Hargrove Road and walking a block or two, my mom got a call from our ambulance driver with news that I was being transported to the hospital. Well, that sent her for a loop because based on our earlier conversation, she didn't even think I was hurt. The driver told her my vital signs were good. My mom later said she could hear me in the background shouting, "I'm fine, Momma, I'm fine."

The driver told them to meet us at the emergency room, which was easier said than done. Since so much of the heavy tornado damage was between our neighborhood and the hospital, all the roads were impassable. What would normally have been a thirty-minute walk took almost three hours by car, weaving their way all over town, even through the ravaged Alberta City area. The sights they saw were like images out of a horror movie—people stumbling around, holding all their possessions in a single suitcase, cars piled on top of each other like building blocks, and sparking power lines wrapped around fallen trees. All the while they had no idea of my condition, other than the "I'm fine" nonsense I had told them on the phone. Nor, for that matter, did they know where Ashley was.

Fortunately, they were able to make it to the hospital just before the National Guard set up a security checkpoint at the front doors. Momma rushed in and told the first person she saw that they needed to see their son, Carson Tinker. The lady told them that everyone had been admitted under code names because so few had identification. My mom asked her to please look for me.

A few minutes later the lady came back: "We found him."

I was still lying on a stretcher in the hallway when Momma and Daddy hurried by. I saw them from behind and yelled, "Hey, over here!"

Whirling around with a look of shock and horror, they couldn't believe what they saw. They were sure the lady had made a mistake. There was no way, they thought, this person could be me. I was so cut up, they didn't recognize me, covered head to toe in dried blood and mud. Debris fragments of all kinds—glass, splinters, rocks, and who knows what else—were lodged in my hair and all over my face.

Once I convinced my parents that I was indeed their one and only son, I went back to saying similar things I had been repeating at Clay and Juli's house. This time they were more like:

"Have they found Ashley?"

"My back hurts." (I was strapped down, lying on a spine board.)

"Have y'all met my nurse, Mandy?"

Momma says I kept saying these things about every three minutes.

At some point during the evening, an ER doctor came to examine my wrist. He said I would probably need surgery, so he sewed it up loosely, just in case. I remember my parents cringing at the sight—my filthy, bloody wrist being sewn up in a dark hallway. It never crossed my mind at the time that this was my long-snapping hand. But my mom sure remembered . . . and made sure the doctor knew it.

Meanwhile, Momma and Daddy were beginning to realize that Ashley hadn't really been on campus or at work like they thought when the tornado hit but had actually been with me—and was apparently still missing. So the next time Dr. Robinson came through to check on me, my mom asked him to look around the hospital to see if by chance Ashley had been admitted. He looked in every room and hallway around the ER, then up and down several floors, but couldn't find her. My parents were starting to fear the worst.

Not only did we not know where Ashley was, but her parents, David and Darlene Harrison, didn't either. And when the tornado touched down, they were more than five hundred miles away in Dallas.

Shortly after they saw the devastating news from Tuscaloosa on television, Ashley's dad started calling her cell phone but didn't get an answer. They figured if Ashley was OK, she would have found a way to let them know. No such call came.

Darlene knows the retired CEO of Southwest Airlines personally, so she desperately called him for flight information to Birmingham. He checked, called her back, and said the next flight was leaving ten minutes from then. Thinking there was no way they could make that flight, Ashley's parents prepared to drive to Tuscaloosa. But just before they left, he called back and said the plane was being held for them because of "weather delays." They rushed to the airport to catch the flight.

After landing in Birmingham, they drove to Tuscaloosa and were at the hospital shortly after midnight. They still didn't know Ashley's whereabouts.

Ashley's grandfather, Marion Perret, and uncle, Marion Perret II, drove up from New Orleans and got to the hospital about the same time as her parents. Since the Perrets had not heard anything definite about Ashley, they went directly to my neighborhood where, along with a couple of firemen, they searched for her through the night. They weren't going anywhere until they found her.

They looked for Ashley until daybreak with no success.

———————

I was put in a private room around 3:00 a.m., absolutely exhausted—physically, mentally, and emotionally. Because of my concussion, they told me not to sleep. Then as soon as they cleared me to sleep, I conked out immediately.

Every time I'd get to sleep, though, some of my friends or teammates or Ashley's sorority sisters would come in. They all wanted to know what they could do regarding Ashley, and I told them all the same thing: "Find her." Several of them had already formed search parties.

Hearing how tight the security was at the door and knowing I had been given a code name when I was admitted, I wondered how all these people were getting up to my room. I later found out they were telling the front desk personnel that I was their brother. I guess those folks at the desk must've thought I had a large family because people were coming in and out all night long.

Jeff Allen, our head football trainer, also stopped in to check on me. From the time the tornado hit, he and many other Athletics Department personnel and coaches had worked tirelessly through the night, trying to contact our more than five hundred athletes. With spotty cell service and power outages all over town, the task of reaching everybody was a near impossibility. But miraculously, all were accounted for with no loss of life.

After finally getting what I think was two to three hours sleep, I woke up around 7:00 a.m., still wearing the same blood-soaked shirt . . . and my bathing suit. I hadn't even been cleaned up yet. My mom was sitting there, and of course the first thing I asked was, "Have they found Ashley? Where's Ashley?"

"Carson," she said . . .

That's when I noticed the tears in her eyes.

"Ashley's gone."

"No," I argued with her. I told her she was wrong. There was no way Ashley hadn't made it. How could she not? We had both been in that closet, hugging each other tightly. How could Payton and Alan and I have escaped—and she hadn't?

"She died of a broken neck, honey. I'm so sorry."

I just lay there, sobbing. I was certainly in no mental condition to hear this, but what else could Momma do? She had no choice but to tell me. She didn't want to risk me hearing about it from someone else, even though she knew I probably couldn't adequately process the gravity of what I was hearing.

Ashley? Gone? It couldn't be. It just couldn't.

She was *right there* with me. How?

What happened?

From what I've learned, Ashley's body was actually discovered while we were still in Clay and Juli's front yard, not long after the tornado had come through. Found in some high grass in between the branches of a fallen tree, just a few yards from where Alan had found me, Ashley didn't have a scratch on her. Darlene said several doctors told her that my being wrapped around her and protecting her the whole time contributed to that.

I sure hope so.

I've also learned that while Clay and Juli were tending to us in their front yard, three guys came out of nowhere and asked if everyone in our group had been accounted for. Juli pulled one of them to the side and told him my girlfriend was missing. She told them where our house had been located and described Ashley to him, all the way down to her fingernail polish.

A few minutes later, the men came back and told Clay and Juli they had found someone matching Ashley's description. They had also run into officer Bob and told him what they had discovered. Bob went over to Ashley's body, confirming the worst, then walked up the street and privately told Juli, yes, he had found someone he felt sure was Ashley. But until she could be positively identified, he wasn't going to say anything on the record. And knowing my physical and emotional condition, he said he sure didn't want me to hear any bad news about Ashley at that time. Then Bob made the arrangements to get us to the hospital.

As we were on our way to DCH, Bob called police headquarters and asked them to expedite the process of removing Ashley's body from the field. So with the help of a neighbor's four-wheeler, they transported her to a facility just a few blocks away. Then at some point that evening, she was taken to the Tuscaloosa V.A. Hospital, where a morgue had been set up.

I appreciate the way Bob took care of Ashley in such a timely manner and the respect he showed her. Although he didn't know us well, we were his neighbors. We had something in common. He just felt a tug on his heart to take extra-special care of her, and I thank him for that.

All during the night, while Ashley's parents, grandfather, and uncle searched for her in the downed trees and debris, she was in the morgue the whole time. Not until around sunrise—when Bob came back to the neighborhood with another Tuscaloosa police officer—did the family know for sure that Ashley hadn't made it. Her uncle identified her from a photo taken at the morgue.

I can't imagine seeing that.

I wish no family ever had to see that.

Shortly before I woke up, my dad, who had been with Ashley's family when Bob and the other officer had come by, confirmed by phone to my mom that our dogs Josey and B had not survived either. They had been found in the field as well, not far from where Ashley's body had been discovered the night before.

Within a couple of hours after the confirmation of Ashley's death, her parents—devastated and exhausted from their all-night search—were in my room, not long after Momma had told me the news.

In anguish and brokenness we all cried on my bed and prayed.

CHAPTER 7

Hurting

As devastated and heartbroken as we were that morning, rocked by the fresh grief over Ashley's death, God soothed our pain with a real-life angel in our midst: Siran Stacy.

Siran's story of sorrow and heartache is well-documented. On November 19, 2007, the former Crimson Tide All-SEC running back suffered a tragedy of epic proportions when his wife and four of his five children were killed in an automobile wreck. Only Siran and his four-year-old daughter Shelly survived.

When Siran walked into my hospital room, it was as if the Lord Himself had appeared. I immediately thought back to my redshirt season in 2008, when he had served as our honorary captain for the Auburn game and Coach Saban presented him a game ball. When Siran reached our sideline following the coin toss, football in hand, he bolted northward, sprinted down the sideline, raised his hands, then hurled the ball high into the end-zone stands.

With everyone knowing what Siran had gone through, you can only imagine how we all felt—fans and players alike—watching him work our crowd into such a frenzy. I have no doubt his emotions were contagious and instrumental in our 36–0 victory.

As I lay in my hospital bed, grieving over the loss of Ashley, Siran's mere presence brought an indescribable peace into the room. More than anything, he just loved on us. He told me he knew what it felt like to wake up and realize the whole world around you is destroyed. He said my pain was being shared by a multitude of people and that prayers were being lifted up for me from all over.

But one thing he said to me struck more deeply than anything else. He reminded me that I was the last person Ashley had been with on earth and that she left this world being embraced by the man she loved. Looking at it from that perspective was a real encouragement to me. It still is. I'm thankful he helped me think of it that way. But I'm also glad for how he challenged me, telling me what I was likely to feel in the days ahead, telling me I couldn't afford to mourn and suffer for long, telling me about some things I needed to do to prepare for life outside these hospital walls— to get ready to step up into these new days and difficulties. To be a man.

I have no doubt that Siran's visit was God ordained. I can't imagine anyone else making the impact he did in that hour or so. Here was a man who lost so much that was precious to him, and yet he was in *my* room, being a blessing to *me*. We were humbled by Siran's servant heart and his testimony of faith in Jesus Christ. Before leaving, he gathered up everyone around my bed and prayed the most powerful, intense, and heartfelt prayer I've ever heard. I'd never felt so weak and so strong, all at the same time.

As I lay in bed that morning with a flood of emotions, I couldn't help but think of our dogs, Josey and B. I expressed my concern to Momma that they were out there in the field with no one to bury them.

Momma called Joe Judge, one of our special teams analysts, who had come by earlier to offer any assistance we needed. She asked if he could round up some guys to give Josey and B a proper burial. Joe got on the phone immediately.

Sometime later that morning, with shovels in hand, my friends and teammates Colin Gallagher, Parker Stinnett, and Spencer Whitfield made the treacherous walk from their house on 13th Street to my neighborhood. Those guys had been to my place many times, but with all the landmarks gone and the surrounding area in shambles, finding my house was difficult.

Once Colin, Parker, and Spencer found what was left of my house, they discovered Josey and B side by side, just as my dad had seen them earlier that morning. As an act of kindness and friendship to Ashley and me, they buried them, marking the two graves with splintered wooden crosses.

Looking through the debris, they also gathered up as much of Josey and B's stuff as they could find—food and water dishes, golf balls, chew toys, leashes, and collars—and created what today has become quite a shrine to our little friends. I know there's no better place on earth for those pups to spend eternity than under the field on which they loved to romp and play.

Believe it or not, I was still as bloody, dirty, and down-right disgusting by mid-morning as I'd been when I was admitted to the hospital the night before. Glass, splinters, and tiny fragments of debris were stuck all over me, even in my ears. I know everybody was awfully busy there. Many of them had probably been working for twenty-four hours straight and had a lot more important things to worry about than whether I was clean or not. But I'm so thankful for Ginger Gilmore, one of our athletic trainers, who came in and tidied me up, not just that first day but every day. With the mess I was in, I took a lot of work.

Other than the countless cuts and scrapes all over my body, the biggest medical concerns were my injured wrist, my concussion, and a large cut on my right ankle. Ginger treated and dressed the wrist and ankle wounds every day. She and the entire training staff took extra-special care of me during my time there.

Early in the afternoon, Coach Saban, Coach Cochran, and Jeff Allen, along with staff photographer Kent Gidley, came to see me. For Coach, his day was already more than seven hours old and would last well into the night.

After arriving at his office around 5:30 a.m., he had immediately begun looking for ways to help. With no power in the building and poor cell phone coverage, he and two staffers had ventured out into the forever-changed land-scape of Tuscaloosa. By 10:00, he was speaking to a group of volunteers at the Ferguson Center, our student hangout. From there, he had gone to the devastated 15th Street areas and given out water, Gatorade, and ice, then traveled across town to the Belk Activity Center at Bowers Park where he met with hundreds of displaced storm victims. After a trip to the UA Student Recreation Center to visit with even more volunteers, he had gone to St. Mathias Church, the official City of Tuscaloosa volunteer location. Later that evening, he returned to the Belk Center and, along with wife Terry, helped feed some seven hundred tornado victims—not only by handing out meals but by footing the entire bill. That's just a small example of what the Sabans did—and are always doing—behind the scenes for people.

I appreciated Coach Saban, Coach Cochran, and Jeff dropping by to check on me. They didn't really know what to say, nor did I. Coach Cochran had met Ashley a couple of times and really liked her. I remember looking at him and saying, "She didn't make it." I was crying.

Coach Cochran cried too.

_____

My four and a half days at DCH were a blur. I really don't remember much about what happened on what day or who came to see me and when. Even my parents say the days ran together.

Sometime on Thursday, the day after the tornado, news began to spread that President Obama was planning a Friday trip to Tuscaloosa to see the tornado damage. Then we heard he may be coming to see me. My first thought was: *Why me? He needs to be spending time out in the community, not in my hospital room.*

I told them to tell him not to come. I didn't want the limelight. There were thousands of people going through what I was going through. I was just one story of many. But I guess because I was an Alabama football player, the president's handlers thought it'd be a good idea for him to drop by, especially since we'd all met him at the White House following the 2009 national championship season. I don't know. And sure enough, Secret Service agents came onto our floor and "swept" the hallways and rooms, confirming the possibility that he and the First Lady might be making an appearance. As it turned out, their two hours in town didn't allow for a visit to the hospital, but it did add to the drama going on all around us.

Arriving in mid-morning on Friday, the president—along with Alabama Governor Robert Bentley and other officials—toured the carnage at 15th Street, McFarland Boulevard, Alberta City, Crescent Ridge Road, and Holt. Stopping along the way to talk to victims, as well as the many volunteers pitching in, the president was quoted as saying, "I've never seen destruction like this."

As much as I don't remember about my hospital stay, I do recall enough about Friday to know one thing—it was the darkest day of my life. Even darker than Wednesday had been.

With the University's final exams cancelled the next week, Ashley's parents wanted her friends, especially her sorority sisters, to be able to pay their last respects before leaving campus. So with only a few hours' notice, they arranged a memorial service for Ashley on Friday afternoon at Tuscaloosa Memorial Chapel Funeral Home.

I insisted on going, not really knowing if I'd be ready for it. My doctors didn't think it was a good idea, either physically or emotionally. Although I didn't have any life-threatening injuries, I was still recovering from the concussion, as well as from countless abrasions all over my body. The most serious issue was my right ankle, where a huge chunk of skin and muscle had been scooped out, as if a rope or cord had been wrapped around the lower inside part of my leg as I flew out of the house and into the field. There's always a chance of infection in such a wound, especially so soon after receiving it, and the thought of my leaving the round-the-clock care of the hospital was problematic for the doctors.

Furthermore, by this time—some thirty-six hours after the tornado—I was dealing with something I later found out to be called Delayed Onset Muscle Soreness, or DOMS. I had never heard of it, and to be honest, I never really focused on it, even though I could certainly feel the pain. I guess my three years under Coach Cochran were paying dividends.

DOMS typically occurs twenty-four to forty-eight hours after the initial event, such as being in a car wreck, or even just when playing backyard tackle football for a few hours or going through a strenuous workout. You may feel fine the next day, but the day afterward you're moaning and groaning. I'm sure everyone has experienced this kind of soreness before at some level.

I probably won't ever know the whole story, but the doctors and hospital folks finally consented and allowed me to go to the memorial service, although for liability reasons I had to be fully discharged and then readmitted afterward. Bill McDonald, our former head athletic trainer and director of sports medicine, arranged for an ambulance to transport us there. My parents as well as my friend, punter Cody Mandell, rode with me. Ginger also came along and never left my side the whole way. I don't know what I would have done without her. She was prepared for anything that might happen during our venture out of the hospital.

From the time I left my room to when I was readmitted less than an hour later, I was in a totally immobilized state in what was basically a bed on wheels. Once inside the funeral home, they tilted me up so I could see Ashley one last time, a memory that'll stay with me forever.

And once I had seen her, I was ready to head back to the hospital. I didn't feel like I could stay any longer. When I got into the ambulance, as soon as the doors closed, everybody in there just cried and cried. The emotions just overwhelmed me.

I don't regret anything about my relationship with Ashley. I never mistreated her or did anything to disrespect her or anything like that. I wasn't the perfect boyfriend, but Lord knows I tried to be. I knew that Ashley was someone special, and I never took her for granted. That's something I hold onto. It gives me peace after everything that happened. I know Ashley is in a better place, and I know she'd be proud of the things I've accomplished.

But most of all, I know I'm a better man spiritually because of the time I spent with her and the influence she had on me. Along with challenging me in school and football, Ashley always challenged me spiritually. She played a big role in leading me to recommit my life to Jesus Christ. That's another thing that brings me peace. Obviously, I wouldn't have chosen to go through what I went through. I would never have wanted to lose her. I was completely content with everything I had and with where I was going. I had Ashley, my dogs, my education, and my teammates. But God had a different plan for me.

And eventually, as hard as we try to fight it, our lives will always bog down if we don't accept what He allows us to go through and endure. We may not like it. We may not have wished it, not in our worst nightmares. But we don't help ourselves or anybody else by staying stuck in our memories and refusing to accept reality. Life can hurt—badly, brutally, unbearably—but we must brace up under it and go on. Somehow.

I know that's what Ashley would've wanted me to do.

I'm so appreciative of all the people who came to see me during my stay at the hospital. Whenever I felt discouraged, I'd look up and someone else would be there to see how I was doing. I'd say fifty to sixty teammates came by at one time or another. A few, like Brandon Gibson and Cody, were there every day.

My roommate Payton came by on Saturday, and my mom took a photo of us, cuts and scrapes and all. Looking at that photo today, I think it was the first time I had smiled since before the tornado. It was really good to see him.

Gary Cramer, our Fellowship of Christian Athletes director, provided another strong source of inspiration for my parents and me, each and every day. Every time he came by, he'd love on us and apply a biblical principle to what had happened and what we were going through. And of course, he wouldn't leave the room without praying for us. He also brought me an FCA T-shirt, which immediately became the only piece of clothing I owned.

My floor nurse, Kim Lancaster, served not only as a great nurse to me but also as an excellent doorkeeper/security guard. You wouldn't believe the number of folks who were just roaming the halls, looking for me or in hopes of seeing some of my teammates. Kim wouldn't let anyone come into my room that I didn't know. She and my ER nurse Mandy were real blessings to me. They helped me get through those tough times.

But even with so many visitors coming in and out all weekend, there was still plenty of alone time—especially at night—when I had nothing to do but think and meditate. Just God and me. During some of those quiet times, I remember thinking how, just as He had put me into this situation, He would get me through it and out of it. I believed there was a reason for this, and I accepted it. I knew there was a reason I was still alive, and I knew there was a reason why Ashley wasn't. To tell you the truth, neither Alan, Payton, Ashley, *nor* I should have made it. Remembering that pile of rubble that used to be our house, I wonder how anybody could have survived.

But we had. It had happened. And for whatever reason, it was becoming clear—through no fault or intention of my own—that I was becoming the "face" of the Tuscaloosa tornado for the Alabama football program and all the fans. I sensed the platform I was about to have, and I knew that people were going to be watching to see how I responded, not only those who were personally affected by the tornado but everybody.

I hadn't been put here because of something I'd done. It had nothing to do with me. This was God using me to do anything He wanted me to do. This was God bringing to life the words of 1 Corinthians 6:19, where Paul writes, "Don't you know that your body is a sanctuary of the Holy Spirit who is in you, whom you have from God? You are not your own."

Indeed, I was not my own; I was His. God had taken just about everything I had—someone I loved very dearly, my health, and my house with everything in it. But He also gave me the resolve to overcome my adversity and to be a blessing to others.

I prayed during the long, silent hours that He would show me how to do it.

———————

Kevin Elko, one of the many motivational speakers Coach Saban brings in for the team—and someone I consider my mentor today—always told us that when things go bad, we have two choices: we can live in *circumstance* or we can live in *vision*.

That principle came back to me often as I lay there in the quiet with God. I could use this horrible circumstance to mope and complain, or I could set an example by overcoming my setback. I could walk around with a constant case of the "poor me's," or I could encourage others who went through the same thing I did. Just as my roommate Payton kept reminding me (in a loving way) that I wasn't the only one who'd been injured or lost a loved one, I could use my situation to help others.

So I resolved, right there in the hospital, to embrace a new normal. I accepted what had happened (my *circumstance*) and made a decision that I was going to live instead in *vision*. I couldn't control what had happened to me, but I could control where I went from there. I could choose my response. And no matter how many times a day this choice needed to be made and remade, I was committed to making the right one.

People were counting on me—a football team, a mom who lost her daughter, students who lost their friends, a community that chose not to accept defeat. Every time I wanted to quit as the days went on, I thought about those people. In my mind I had a team on my back, families on my back, victims and survivors on my back. I would not be denied what I wanted—my vision.

And it wasn't all about me. The people in Tuscaloosa were counting on all of us, on all my teammates. People needed us—a school, a community, a town, a city, a state. I knew God had established a plan for me, and this was it: to inspire, motivate, and challenge people. I was on a mission. I'm *still* on a mission. That's where our circumstances are supposed to lead us.

As I said at the beginning of this book, God gives us comfort so we can give that comfort to others. That's my mission now, to show God's comfort to others. I believe that's why I went through what I had to go through—so I could help others, so I could be a blessing to them. I believe that is God's plan for me.

Jeremiah 29:11 says, "For I know the plans I have for you . . . plans for your welfare, not for disaster, to give you a future and a hope." God has a plan for everyone.

When I go and speak to students, that's what I always tell them. I tell them I've sat in the same seat they're sitting in now, looking at a speaker. I'm no different than they are. The only difference is that God had a different plan for me, just as He has a unique plan for them, just as He has a unique plan for everybody.

Coach Cochran once told me, "Before there was a you, there was a God-thing for you to do. He designed you to do it." And every time I would start to get worn down in the days ahead—from rehab, from practice, from workouts, from the media, from the whole thing—I'd think about what he told me that day in his office.

God has a plan for me.

God has a plan for you.

And He expects us to live in that vision.

CHAPTER 8

Healing

You'd think after four and a half days in the hospital, especially after what I'd been through, I'd be ready to knock down the doors to get out of there.

Not so.

On Monday morning the doctors approved my release, but I really didn't want to leave. The hospital had become my safe haven. I honestly didn't feel ready to face the stark realities that existed outside those walls. Everybody who came to see me talked about how awful it was out there—the damage and destruction; the homes, businesses, and churches destroyed; how Tuscaloosa's landscape had been forever altered. I didn't want to see it. I didn't know what was out there, and I didn't want to know.

Even after being released and getting into my parents' car, I laid down in the backseat so I wouldn't see anything on the way out of town. To make sure, I even asked them to drive a route that avoided most of the tornado damage.

I knew I'd have to return to Tuscaloosa one day, but until then all I could think about was getting to my parents' house in Birmingham. I longed for rest and sleep.

I hadn't been home any time at all before Josh Maxson in our Athletics Communications office called me. He said that several media outlets—the *Today Show*, ESPN, and several magazines—had requested interviews with me. But I didn't want to talk to anybody, in fear of saying something I would later regret. I wanted to wait as long as possible before talking to the media. After all, physically I was a wreck. Only five days removed from the tornado, with cuts and scrapes from head to toe, my body was not ready for prime time.

My rest lasted all of about two days.

As much as I wanted to stay at home, I knew my challenges were just beginning. With the start of football practice only three months away, getting back to normal—and when I say "normal," I mean *football player* normal—was first and foremost on my mind. So on Wednesday, one week after the tornado, my arduous task of rehabilitation began at Champion Sports Medicine, located at St. Vincent's Hospital in Birmingham.

Champion is the rehab division of the Andrews Sports Medicine and Orthopaedic Center. Famed orthopedic surgeon Dr. James Andrews, the center's founder, is the choice of many of the world's elite athletes, especially those with knee, elbow, or shoulder injuries. Dr. Andrews' patient list reads like a who's who of stars, including Brett Favre, Tom Brady, Drew Brees, Troy Aikman, Emmett Smith, Peyton Manning, and Adrian Peterson from football; Shaquille O'Neal, Allen Iverson, Michael Jordan, and Charles Barkley from basketball; and John Smoltz, Albert Pujols, and Roger Clemens from baseball. Even wrestler John Cena, golfer Jack Nicklaus, and multisport star Bo Jackson—whom I consider

My propensity to laugh started at the young age of three months.

At eight months, with my dad wearing his vintage early-1990s Bama hat.

Just a couple of weeks before my second birthday, I dressed in full Alabama football gear for Halloween.

At age three, enjoying a rare snow day in Decatur.

By the fireplace at Christmas, with visions of football dancing in my head.

In the first grade, on my first flag football team. After getting busted in the nose on the opening day of practice, I wanted to quit on the spot, but my parents wouldn't let me. It was a great life lesson that prepared me for tougher times down the road.

For church friend Nina Cline's 100th birthday celebration, she asked me to be her "prince." My parents were notified after her death that she had left me some money for my college education, which helped tremendously my freshman year when we were paying out-of-state tuition.

At age nine, with my parents on a family camping trip to Fontana Dam, North Carolina.

All-Star baseball photo. From early on, my parents were always involved in my sports teams.

Proudly displaying my certificate for winning a city-wide poetry contest in the fifth grade.

My first year of tackle football in the fifth grade.

In my second year of football, I switched to No. 51, which would become my number while playing for the Crimson Tide.

Smiles were aplenty after hitting a home run while playing for the Giants. My dad was undergoing his cancer treatments at the time.

Chillin' with my dog Peanut and my dad.

My sophomore season at Riverdale High School in Murfreesboro, Tennessee.

In 2006, during my junior season at Riverdale, my dad took me to the Alabama-Ole Miss game in Tuscaloosa. Somehow, someway, I got Joe Namath to sign my No. 12 jersey. From that day forward, my goal was to play for the Tide. Less than two years later, my dream came true.

With my buddy and Riverdale teammate Michael Pope (above) following our high school graduation. Shortly after the tornado three years later, Michael and David Sumrall (another Riverdale teammate, pictured below) came to Birmingham and helped me navigate through a tough time in my life.

Wearing a tux while holding a football was a Riverdale senior portrait tradition for the senior football players.

Ashley (right), with her parents
Darlene and David Harrison.

Ashley and our black lab
Bottega, whose name we
immediately shortened to B.

Our awesome dogs, Josey and B.

Josey and B at my parents' house in Birmingham.
Every time they would lie down together, B would
place her paw on Josey.

April 27, 2011, the day we were forever changed.

Photo by Clay Carter

As far as I know, this is the only photo of me (wrapped in the blue blanket) within an hour after the tornado. After frantically searching for Ashley with no success, our neighbors Clay and Juli Carter tended to me and my roommates Payton Holley (left) and Alan Estis (right) in their driveway. Juli is standing behind me. Across the street is just a small snapshot of what's left of the field.

My house was literally lifted off its foundation and dropped across the street. The red car belonged to my roommate Alan Estis. The blue Jeep was mine. Ironically, our house was completely destroyed, yet the aluminum storage shed at the end of the driveway was, for the most part, undamaged. (Last time I checked, it's still there today.)

Taken from behind my house looking northeast, my totaled Jeep (far right), Ashley's white SUV, the house's foundation, some house debris, and the field across the street.

My field of dreams, where Josey and B chased my golf balls, was ripped to pieces.

My house debris, across the street some 50–75 yards away.

More debris, including a portion of red carpet from my den. The destroyed house behind our debris is in the Glendale Gardens neighborhood.

The morning after the tornado, friends of Ashley's constructed a memorial, which stands to this day.

Parker Stinnett (in red cap with shovel), Colin Gallagher (not pictured), and Spencer Whitfield (not pictured) buried our beloved dogs, Josey and B.

The memorial to Josey and B, complete with their dishes, collars, leashes, and toys.

On the day after the tornado, Jason and Maria Hargrove—friends of Clay and Juli Carter—found my muddied BCS National Championship jersey amidst the rubble of my house.

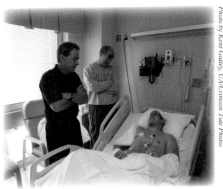

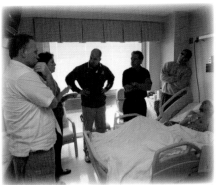

Midway through a long day of serving others, Coach Saban and Coach Cochran offered encouragement in my hospital room.

My mom and dad, along with head trainer Jeff Allen, Coach Saban, and Coach Cochran.

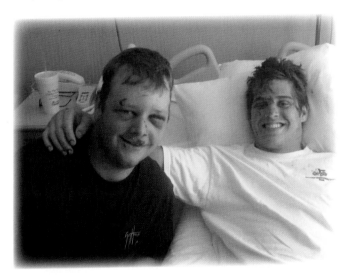

A Saturday morning hospital visit from my roommate Payton Holley put a smile on my face, my first since the tornado. The FCA T-shirt I'm wearing, brought to me by our FCA director Gary Cramer, was at this time the only piece of clothing I owned.

A couple of months after the tornado, the Alabama football team had a workday in tornado-ravaged Holt. Although I was physically limited in what I could do, I'm so glad I was there.

The Walk of Champions prior to every home game is a highlight of every player who wears the Crimson and White.

Post-game prayers, such as this one following the 2011 victory over Arkansas, were always so meaningful to me.

During Alabama's bye week in 2011, I was asked to flip the coin prior to a Riverdale High School game in Murfreesboro. Following the coin toss, Principal Tom Nolan (left) and baseball coach Barry Messer presented to me a framed Riverdale jersey.

Preparing to snap for a field goal attempt in the 2011 "Game of the Century" versus LSU.

At the annual football awards banquet in December 2011, Athletics Academics advisor Lance Walker (back row, second from right) presented "Commitment to Academic Excellence" awards to, left to right, Mark Barron, Cyrus Kouandjio, Barrett Jones, Trent Richardson, D. J. Fluker, and me.

Following the 2011 regular season, on behalf of the Alabama football team, I was honored to accept the Disney Spirit Award from Faron Kelley, Disney Sports' director of marketing.

With the Disney Spirit Award at the Home Depot College Football Awards show in Orlando, Florida.

In the BCS game against LSU, blocking for one of Jeremy Shelley's record five made field goals in our 21–0 victory.

The sweet kiss of victory. After what we'd been through in 2011, holding that crystal ball was an answered prayer.

2012 BCS National Championship team photo.
I'm on the second row, tenth from the right.

"Snapping" the crystal football at our National Championship Celebration in Bryant-Denny Stadium in January 2012.

With Alabama Governor Robert Bentley in his office prior to his February 2012 "State of the State" address, where he recognized me as one of the many Tuscaloosa and Alabama residents who persevered through adversity.

Team trip to the White House in April 2012.

With President Barack Obama in front of the White House.

For a naming right in our locker room inside the Mal M. Moore Athletics Facility, my good friend Warner Moore III made a donation to the Crimson Tide Foundation in memory of Ashley.

Going downfield with Cody Mandell (#29) and Tana Patrick (#11) after a punt in our 2012 comeback win over LSU in Baton Rouge.

On the bench with my friend Jeremy Shelley in the 2012 LSU game.

With my parents and Coach Saban at Senior Day in Bryant-Denny Stadium, just before the 2012 Auburn game.

Preparing to snap against Auburn in my final Bryant-Denny game.

Photo by Kent Gidley, UA/Crimson Tide Photos

Celebrating with 2012 SEC Championship Game Offensive MVP Eddie Lacy following his 181-yard rushing performance against Georgia in our 32–28 victory.

In my five seasons at Alabama, I was blessed to be a part of two SEC Championship teams and three BCS National Championship teams.

Sprinting downfield in the BCS National Championship Game against Notre Dame.

Photo by Kent Gidley, UA/Crimson Tide Photos

Receiving a bear hug from defensive coordinator Kirby Smart following our 42–14 win over the Fighting Irish.

Above, working with Habitat for Humanity and Calvary Baptist Church on the "Get Jackie Home for Christmas" project. At right, with my mom outside Ms. Jackie's new house.

Following the 2012 season, I participated in the Senior Bowl in Mobile, as well as the Raycom College Football All-Star Classic in Montgomery. And every time I signed an autograph for a kid, I couldn't help but think back to my days growing up, always wanting to play for the Crimson Tide.

Following an Alabama softball game, Baron Huber (far left), Wesley Britt (in rear), and I were among many former Alabama football and softball alumni to play the Wounded Warrior Amputee Softball Team in an exhibition game. The Wounded Warrior's team goal is to show other amputees and the general population that through extensive rehabilitation and training, they are able to express their desires and perform the sport they love.

With my new jersey No. 46, realizing my NFL dream as a player for the Jacksonville Jaguars.

Photo by Rick Wilson/Jacksonville Jaguars

one of the greatest athletes of all-time—have sought out Dr. Andrews and his associates for their care.

Having someone like Dr. Andrews and his partner Dr. Lyle Cain as our team orthopedic surgeons at Alabama is quite a plus for us. It's just another example of the Athletics Department offering the absolute best to its athletes, whether you're talking about facilities, academic support, coaching, counseling, or injury rehab. Believe me, I benefitted from all of them during my five years in Tuscaloosa.

Before I could get started on my first day of rehab, however, Dr. Cain first needed to remove about twenty staples from three or four cuts in my head. To be honest, I didn't even remember getting those staples put in. I guess it was early on in my hospital stay—before I was completely aware of what all was happening.

As I was leaving Dr. Cain's office to head downstairs to rehab, a young girl in the waiting room caught my eye. The pain and sadness on her face were obvious. I sensed immediately that her life had been forever changed by the tornado, just like mine. Asking the staff, I found out she had lost one of her parents in the Jefferson County portion of the same tornado that ravaged Tuscaloosa. So before I left, I went over, introduced myself, and we chatted for a few minutes. I encouraged her to be strong and to think positive thoughts. She smiled. It reminded me again: *be a blessing*. I knew I'd have a million more opportunities to do it if I'd just be looking for them.

And they started right then.

———————

My daytime home for the next few weeks was at Champion. Five days a week, for several hours a day, rehabbing became my life.

I don't remember much about my first day, other than I didn't want to be there. My certified athletic trainer, Kirk Kaps, told me later that in my first rehab session I didn't say a word. I just did what they said. Perhaps my silence was from the pain I was experiencing. Maybe it was the exhaustion from not being able to sleep, from staying up till four or five every night. Perhaps it was the uncertainty of what lay ahead for me on the football field. Perhaps it was grief over Ashley that I was still trying to process. Whatever it was, I'm glad I wasn't responsible for getting there each day because I couldn't have done it. I thank my mom for waking me up and making me go.

One blessing, though, that came from those long nights of insomnia were the hours and hours I spent reading my Bible. Growing up, of course, I had read the stories and verses in Sunday school or in Bible studies, but I had never read the Bible straight through, from cover to cover. However, in the torment and tedium of those long nights, in solitude with the Word, I could really feel God speaking to me.

And I needed it. During my entire rehabilitation process, I was forced to make a choice—several times a day—whether to focus on the positive or on the negative, whether to work to get better or to give in and get worse. Like Coach Cochran used to tell us, the world is full of "average." He'd always shout, "Who strives to be average? It's easy to be easy!"

My rehabilitation centered on four main areas: the wrist fracture on my snapping hand, regaining my general flexibility, full strength restoration, and the open wound on my lower leg. All of them were important, of course, but the need to recover my long-snapping form was primary to me. And since no exercise could get me ready for snapping better than snapping itself, I was fortunate to be able to do that in a state-of-the-art lab at the nearby American Sports Medicine Institute. This is where baseball-pitching biomechanics are analyzed to study injury treatment and injury prevention. Some two thousand baseball pitchers—and now one college long snapper—have used it. Having that kind of facility right there was so beneficial. It sure felt good to snap again.

Most of my exercises were for overall strength and flexibility. My lower body exercises were the same type as someone with torn ACLs would do, emphasizing my quads, hamstrings, hips, and calf muscles. Although I wasn't able to be at Coach Cochran's sessions in Tuscaloosa, I was sure getting a workout in Birmingham.

Most of Dr. Andrews's and Dr. Cain's "superstar" patients fly into Birmingham, have their surgeries, then fly back for rehab with their team athletic trainers. But if time allows, some stay in Birmingham and rehab at Champion. Although I hadn't been through any kind of surgery myself, I was able to be in a rehab group primarily for professional and college athletes recovering from surgeries and trying to get back into playing shape. In our group was former Alabama fullback Tim Castille of the Kansas City Chiefs; Leonard Weaver, an All-Pro fullback for the Philadelphia Eagles; former Kentucky player and NBA free agent Kelenna Azubuike; and Mo Finley, a former UAB basketball player who was playing professionally in Italy. Each of those guys was a real blessing to me. They were all going through adversity, so we had a lot in common.

Rehab at Champion was tough, but we did have some fun times. We'd goof around trying to make trick shots with a Nerf basketball. We'd watch *Let's Make a Deal* and *The Price Is Right* every day. I was usually there from 9:00 in the morning to 1:00 or so in the afternoon, then my dad and I would go to lunch.

Perhaps the highlight of being around those guys was that all of us were what I'd call "religious." We'd talk about God and spiritual issues every day. It did me a lot of good to see these professional athletes talk so openly about their faith. All of them knew Scripture and would quote it regularly. I don't know if I made any impact on them while they were there, but they sure made an impact on me.

Especially impressive to me was Leonard Weaver, who in 2010 had become the highest paid fullback in NFL history. An opening-game knee injury had brought him to the Andrews Center and to Champion Sports Medicine.

One thing Leonard said that has always stuck with me was about tithing—how he gave a minimum of 10 percent of his income to his church. He talked about the importance of being faithful to that regular discipline of giving, which for him would be figured on *millions* of dollars. I thought that was so cool because some people chase after money and fame, get it, and are never satisfied. Then there's a guy like Leonard who has the money and fame; yet he's perfectly content.

The Bible says, in Philippians 4:11–12: "I have learned to be content in whatever circumstances I am. I know both how to have a little, and I know how to have a lot. In any and all circumstances I have learned the secret of being content—whether well fed or hungry, whether in abundance or in need."

I can't read those verses any longer without thinking of Leonard Weaver.

As good as the rehab was going on my wrist, flexibility, and strength, I couldn't say the same about the open wound on my leg. Despite daily cleaning treatments, it wasn't showing much progress. It looked like somebody had taken a divot out of it with a nine iron.

In my second week of rehab, Dr. Cain said, "Carson, I don't think we can do anything more with your leg. You're going to need help from a specialist." I guess I was naïve; I just assumed it would grow back and heal right up.

Dr. Cain referred me to Dr. Michael Beckenstein, a plastic surgeon located within the St. Vincent's complex. The first time I spoke with "Dr. B," I noticed he was so full of energy. He was almost a little too much for me at first. I remember thinking to myself, *How long am I going to have to deal with this guy?* But now I love him to death, and I know beyond the shadow of a doubt I would not be where I am today if it weren't for him.

Dr. B has a heart of gold and is widely known for his plastic surgery work. Some of his cases that have received national attention include restoring to full health a young Filipino boy with severe burns on his arm and leg, a case referred to by the media as a "plastic surgery miracle." Another well-documented case was his reconstruction of the torso of a girl who had been dragged under a school bus. He was able to restore her appearance successfully, a case written about in a *People* magazine article.

After watching Dr. B in action, I knew I was in good hands.

Several times a week following my rehab sessions, I would go to his office for treatment. I was still beaten up, sore, and emotionally broken. The first day I saw him, he cleaned out the wound on my leg and started to examine it. I couldn't feel anything in that area of my leg since whatever happened to it had taken the nerve endings with it.

He then put me on something called a wound vacuum, a contraption hooked to my belt with tubes going down the outside of my leg to the wound. Although I knew its purpose—to force out all the junk and help pull the tissue and muscle back even with the rest of my leg—I hated it. I had to wear it for a couple of months, even when I was sleeping. The only time I took it off was for showers. That thing drove me crazy.

But being recovered is always worth the pain and frustration to get there. And that wound vacuum, along with Dr. B's treatments, did the trick. My leg showed great improvement by the time I got back to campus in June. The treatments would continue into the season.

As much as Dr. B helped me physically, he was an even bigger influence on me emotionally. Every session with him, I'd come away with so much encouragement. About a week into my treatments, he shared with me a video clip from the World War II film *Saving Private Ryan*, starring, among others, Tom Hanks as Captain John Miller and Matt Damon as Private James Ryan. Miller's mission in the movie is to find and bring home Private Ryan, whose three brothers had already been killed in battle. Ryan is indeed found but with great cost—the lives of many of Miller's men. Near the end, a dying Miller tells Ryan, in probably the most memorable and dramatic scene from the film, to "earn this! Earn it!"—to live a life worthy of the lives sacrificed to rescue him. Miller was saying, in so many words, "Private Ryan, now go make a difference in someone's life!"

After showing me the clip, Dr. B looked at me and said, "There's a reason you're here, Carson, just like there's a reason Ashley isn't here. Don't worry about what that reason is right now. Just know you're here for a reason, and you have to earn it. Earn it. You lived through something you shouldn't have lived through. No one in your house should be alive, including you. Your job now is to go earn it."

I know as a Christian, we can't do anything to earn God's love for us. He gives us His mercy as an act of pure grace, and we receive it because we have nothing equal to offer Him in return. But at the same time, we do have a responsibility to put the life He's given us into practice. And seeing that movie scene reinforced what I had already decided—to give back in memory of those who had given their lives in the tornado. To do something for somebody else. To concentrate on the positive, not the negative. To live in vision, not circumstance. To be a blessing.

I was sure of that.

The only conflict I felt inside was that I really didn't want the attention that might come from it. I felt like the media had overplayed my story. I was just one of many who were suffering. Six students, including Ashley, had been killed in the storm, and their families were going through a lot more pain and agony than I was, no matter how badly my losses and injuries hurt, both emotionally and physically.

I remember saying to one of my classmates around this time: "Look, I'm just a long snapper. I enjoy being the invisible man. I don't like this attention. If I could just get through with school, help as many people as I can, and fly completely under the radar, that'd be fine with me."

He said, "You know, that's one of the reasons people like your story so much, Carson, because you're just an average guy."

After all, I am. I'm not superathletic, not very talented, not a five-star prospect. "You're just like me," he said. "You're just a normal guy."

That really hit home because, after all, I *am* just a normal guy.

And most people who are the greatest blessings to others—they're just normal people too.

But within a few weeks, this "normal guy" was featured in a *Sports Illustrated* cover story, along with several other Alabama athletes impacted by the tornado.

Although I had declined some earlier interviews from national media, the opportunity to be in *Sports Illustrated* was different. My decision served two purposes. First, it gave me a chance to get my side of the story out. I didn't want people to take what they had seen on television or heard through the grapevine and twist it in any way. I felt like I needed to tell the story from my perspective, hopefully in a positive, inspirational way. I wanted to show people how God was working through me. I prayed this opportunity would help me do that.

Second, having such a well-respected magazine as *Sports Illustrated* as my platform made it all the better. So when Josh from our Athletics Communications office called and ran it by me, I said I'd do it. He told me that Lars Anderson, an *SI* writer based in Birmingham, would be writing the article.

A couple of weeks after the tornado, Lars and I met in Tuscaloosa in the Crimson Tide Foundation's Donor Hall of Recognition in the south end of Bryant-Denny Stadium.

They wanted to take photos of me at what was left of my house and around my neighborhood, but I didn't want to do that. At that time, I had no desire to go back there.

Lars and I talked for more than an hour. I didn't want to tell him just a little bit at a time; I wanted to do it all at once. I told him everything that happened, how I had accepted it, and how through my experience I wanted to bless others. I expressed to him that I knew I couldn't change what had happened, but God had a reason for it. I told him my role and mission from this point forward was to be an inspiration to people.

Before the article was published, Lars allowed me to double- and triple-check it for accuracy. That's probably a no-no in journalism, but the subject matter was so sensitive he wanted to make sure everything was exactly right. During this editing process, I hated reading it over and over, remembering it, rehashing it, but I really felt like it needed to be written.

Within a couple of weeks, my story—along with several other first-person accounts—came to life in an *SI* article entitled "Terror, Tragedy, and Hope in Tuscaloosa." On the front cover was my former teammate and current Arizona Cardinal Javier Arenas, his battered neighborhood serving as the backdrop.

Besides my and Javi's stories, Lars penned the harrowing experiences of gymnast Kayla Hoffman and baseball players Josh Rosecrans and Nate Kennedy. Although I had already read my portion of the story prior to publication, I wasn't aware of the others' stories until the magazine came out. I was especially intrigued by Josh and Nate's story of having Psalm 121:7–8 written on an index card taped to their bathroom mirror. The verses read this way:

The LORD will protect you from all harm;
He will protect your life. The LORD will
protect your coming and going both now
and forever.

Just before the tornado ripped through their house, Josh and Nate threw a mattress over themselves and took refuge in a bathtub. Thirty seconds later they crawled out, unharmed. The only walls left standing were those of the bathroom they were in.

Still taped to the mud-splattered mirror was the Bible verse.

CHAPTER 9

New Season

I have no idea how many people read the *Sports Illustrated* article, but it must've been a bunch. Folks would come up to me almost every day and tell me how sorry they were. I appreciated their concern, but at the same time it was hard for the memory to keep coming up again and again. It's not like I'll ever forget it, but part of me—even with the article out there—just didn't want to think about it. And I sure didn't want people feeling sorry for me.

They'd start by asking, "Aren't you the guy who lost his girlfriend in the tornado?"

Yes, I am. That's how people came to know me. It became a weight I was forced to carry—something I'll always have to live with. But I hated talking about the tornado, for obvious reasons. Most people who asked about it didn't understand—*couldn't* understand—what I was going through.

Even people who didn't know about my connection with the tornado would often ask, when they noticed the wound vacuum I was carrying around, "What's *that*?" I didn't want to be rude, so I'd answer, "Well, it's hooked up to my leg to help heal a wound. I was in the tornado."

"Oh, what happened?"

"I was thrown out of my house."

"Oh, man, are you OK?"

"Yeah."

"Everybody else OK?"

"No, my girlfriend and my two dogs died."

And then they'd feel bad for asking me, and I would feel bad for making them feel bad. It was awkward, to say the least. Because of this, I now know never to ask questions like that about someone. When I see anybody in a goofy-looking cast or a crazy brace or something, I just try to make them laugh.

So, yes, on one hand, talking about the tornado was painful. But on the other hand, God was doing so many things with me for the good that I wanted people to know. That's one of the reasons I decided to write this book. I wanted people to know that God can take you, no matter where you are, and use it for good.

I thought back to that story from Joseph's life in the Old Testament, where he told his brothers who had sold him into slavery, not knowing it would eventually lead him to become part of the royalty in Egypt: "You planned evil against me; God planned it for good to bring about the present result— the survival of many people" (Gen. 50:20).

I knew I couldn't go out and literally save lives, but I could do one thing, and that was to be a blessing to other people.

Starting by becoming the best conditioned football player I could be.

———————

In early June, I headed back to Tuscaloosa with one thing in mind, at least physically speaking—getting ready to play football again. My four weeks of rehab at Champion Sports in Birmingham had been beneficial, and I'll always be grateful for the work of Kirk and his staff. But in order for me to get my mind right, I needed to be in Tuscaloosa. Fewer than three months remained before our home opener against Kent State, and I knew our coaches were counting on me to be ready.

Rehab through the summer was under the watchful eyes of Ginger Gilmore, Jeff Allen, and Rodney Brown in our training room. Believe me, I wanted to be out there with my teammates during summer workouts, even in the 100-degree heat, but I just wasn't ready. I would have given anything to be out running 110s and doing all that crazy conditioning with Coach Cochran, but I couldn't. About all I could do was snap the ball. I was still so stiff and weak.

Not only was I rehabbing my injuries and trying to get into shape; I still had my leg to deal with. Although the tissue was getting better, I still had an open wound about the diameter of a Coke can. We didn't want it to scab over because it wouldn't heal properly, so we kept it wrapped up in what's called a wet-to-dry bandage, which clings to the skin cells inside the wound so you can pull them out. Whenever I'd change the dressing, I was supposed to scrub my leg until it started bleeding. This promoted growth in the leg. And thankfully, since the nerve endings down there still weren't sending pain signals to my brain, I couldn't feel any of it.

In many ways, I feel like my experience with the tornado can be defined by what the treatment of this wound required.

First, it was a process. I had to take care of my wound every single day. And though it didn't get better overnight, it did get a little better each day. I'd take a picture of it after every treatment, and I could never tell a difference from day to day. But if I looked at the pictures a week at a time, I could see the wound becoming smaller and smaller.

Second, the adversity made me stronger. If I had sat around and done nothing to my leg, it would never have gotten better. But the daily scrubbing and aggravating made it bleed and promoted healthy growth and stronger tissue.

Finally, the wound process taught me perseverance. It was hard to change that bandage and scrub my leg three or four times a day. But I trusted in the process and knew it was what I needed to do to get better.

Process. Strength. Perseverance through adversity. I would need all three of these and more to get back where I wanted to be, in all the ways God was enabling me to carry out His plan for my life.

———————

Being back in Tuscaloosa allowed me the chance to venture out into the community and participate in several tornado relief efforts, including a football player workday at SOMA Church in Holt. About fifty of us raked and hauled off debris. At first, due to my physical limitations, I was a bit apprehensive about going, but I'm sure glad I went ahead anyway. It was all about being a blessing to others.

I can't begin to express how proud I was of all our Crimson Tide athletes and their contributions to the relief efforts throughout the summer. Everywhere I turned, they were helping. Besides the workdays, my football teammates distributed Gatorade, protein bars, Muscle Milk, snacks, water, and T-shirts all over town.

I mentioned earlier Josh Rosecrans and Nate Kennedy losing their house, but they were only two of thirteen members of the Alabama baseball team who were displaced. Once all those guys found housing, their efforts turned toward helping with cleanup in the 15th Street and McFarland area.

Basketball coach Anthony Grant established the Sweet Home Fund to aid in rebuilding and recovery, and his players went around clearing debris and helping salvage personal belongings from folks' houses. The men's golf team distributed supplies and cleared debris while the women's team assisted in food and water distribution in the Alberta City area.

The Alabama gymnasts—three of whom lost their houses in the storm—delivered toys and supplies to elementary schools, unloaded donated supplies, and participated in a relief fund-raiser on the *Hey Coach* radio show.

Our rowing team cut trees and branches and helped families move furniture out of their houses, while our volleyball team spent hours helping in the hard-hit Holt area.

The soccer team was all over the place—helping Samaritan's Purse (a Christian relief agency headed by Franklin Graham), clearing debris, distributing food and supplies, laying tarps, volunteering at the Salvation Army, working at a vet clinic to help reunite pets and owners, and helping feed a group of athletes from Notre Dame who spent their fall break in Tuscaloosa volunteering.

The softball team invested long hours at Temporary Emergency Services. Pat Greenwell, our diving coach, operated his tractor for eight to ten hours a day in the Holt area. One of our men's tennis players served as a Spanish interpreter between victims and relief workers at Tuscaloosa Emergency Services, while some of his teammates held fund-raisers in their hometowns. Women's tennis team members assisted in food and toy distribution in Holt, while many of our track and field athletes helped out with the Convoy of Hope's distribution of more than 200,000 pounds of food, water, and supplies.

I was especially proud of our late Athletics Director Mal Moore and the Athletics Department. They donated $1 million to the UA Acts of Kindness Fund, a charitable account established by the University to assist students, faculty, and staff who were impacted by the tornado. And of course, Coach Saban and Ms. Terry really stepped up with their personal contributions, as well as with donations from their Nick's Kids Fund.

Help was coming from every sector of the Alabama athletics family, as well as from many other folks around the school and community. It was so inspiring to see. People came together, and our town and campus were slowly coming back.

———————

Physical labor, although hard on the body, can serve as good therapy, especially after such a traumatic event as we all experienced. There comes a time, however, when *mental* therapy is needed as well—moments when we corporately reflect and remember.

One such opportunity occurred in early June, when I attended a "Spirit of Tuscaloosa" candlelight vigil downtown. It was a nice way to honor all those who had lost their lives in the tornado.

At the end of the event, they showed a video montage of the tornado and all the relief efforts. It was difficult to watch. Near the end, I saw a lot of people crying, including a family right near me. I didn't know who they were. I went over to them and said, "Look, I don't know who you are or why you're here, and you probably don't know who I am, but I'm sorry. God will get you through this." We just sat there and cried. I was holding their whole family, and they were holding me, and we were just crying. Then the man said, "I know who you are, and I'm sorry, too. We're here for Loryn Brown."

As it turned out, the man I was talking to was Shannon Brown, the former Alabama football player who lost his daughter Loryn in the storm. I had heard reports that she had fled to her basement as the tornado approached, and the whole house collapsed on her. She was in what she thought was the safest place in the whole city.

I couldn't help but think back to the day of the storm, when I kept telling Ashley, Payton, and Alan that if a tornado comes, we'd break into our neighbor's house and get in their basement. But the basement of that house collapsed during the tornado, and if we'd been in there, all of us would have died. I'm sure of it. As unsafe as that closet of ours became when the tornado spun up right over our heads, it was probably the safest of all places to be at the moment.

I don't know what that means, really, but I know we did our best to deal with the limited choices available. And as costly as it was—especially for Ashley and her parents—I know God led us to take refuge there. I know He was still in control, even in those horrible minutes. And I know He wants us to keep trusting Him, even with things we don't understand.

It's all part of the healing process.

———————

Later that summer, along with evangelist Scott Dawson, I spoke at a "Restoration of Hope" event in Arab, a small town in north Alabama that was also hit hard by the tornado outbreak of April 27. Several area churches combined their congregations and choirs for a two-hour remembrance.

I had developed sort of a set speech I'd give whenever I spoke somewhere, but when I got up to the stage that night, I didn't really know what to say. Speaking to them was not like any place I had ever been. These people had lost family members, their houses, everything. They were broken, just as I was.

But they were still worshipping God, just as Job did when he was at his lowest. I remember thinking of that verse in John 9 where Jesus explained to the crowd how a certain man's blindness, when encountered by the healing touch of God, had become an opportunity to show what God could do in a person's life. "This came about," Jesus said, "so that God's works might be displayed in him" (John 9:3). These people's lives in Arab had been torn to pieces, and yet here they were—wanting God to get praise from their tragedy, wanting to be transformed by what they'd endured so they could come out on the other end even better, even stronger.

When I finally found the words, I told them what had happened to me and how we can't control what happens. But we can always control how we respond. I think we all experienced a special touch from God that night.

Another opportunity to share my story came at Cornerstone Baptist in Sardis City, a little community near Boaz. At the first part of the service when everybody was shaking hands, an older man wearing a Hawaiian shirt, looking like he'd been strung out for two weeks, came up to me and said, "I just lost my wife, and I want to know how you got over what you went through. Not ten minutes go by that I don't think about her."

"Just hear me out," I told him. "Listen to what I'm about to say."

As I began my message, I pointed to that guy and said, "I'm going to pour out my heart in this service just for you." I didn't even talk about the tornado. My whole theme was about living in vision instead of circumstance. I told them we have to want to get better. Just as that man will never forget his wife, I'll never forget Ashley and everything I went through, but I will not let these events—as horrible as they've been—determine my future.

That guy came up to me afterwards and said, "I really appreciate what you said to me. I will never forget that."

Again, 2 Corinthians 1:3–4 says it best:

> Bless be the God and Father of our Lord
> Jesus Christ, the Father of mercies and
> the God of all comfort. He comforts us in
> all our affliction, so that we may be able
> to comfort those who are in any kind of
> affliction, through the comfort we ourselves
> receive from God.

God gave me comfort in all that I went through. And I in turn gave God's comfort to that man.

That's the kind of blessing I want to be.

———————

"Earn it."

That phrase from *Saving Private Ryan* lodged in my head the entire summer before camp. My vision was to play football, and I was committed to that vision. Through God, my hard work, and dedication, I was going to see my vision fulfilled.

Proverbs 16:3 says, "Commit your activities to the LORD, and your plans will be achieved." Being committed to something has nothing to do with ability, talent, or physical prowess. It's all a mind-set. How much does it mean to you? My vision meant everything to me.

I knew I was committed. But in order to put my commitment into actionable words, I decided to *write down* my goals in my own handwriting and hang them in my locker.

- I want to be the best snapper in college football.
- No one will give more effort than I will.
- I will outwork every long snapper in the country.

I looked at these goals every day. It's one thing to *think* about doing something or to see something another person is doing and want to accomplish it in our own lives. But when we put it in our own handwriting, we're making ourselves an implied promise. If we don't fulfill it, we're not just passing up an opportunity. We're cheating on ourselves. We're letting ourselves down. And I was not about to do that.

Summer conditioning gets hard. The west Alabama sun is nothing to play with. It gets easy to go through the motions as the scorching hot days build up. But whenever I felt like quitting—even during my limited conditioning capabilities at that time—I would look back at those goals I had written, the things I wanted to accomplish for myself, and I could feel my dedication and commitment come roaring back.

It had already been a season to remember before I even started thinking about what was coming around the corner. But I needed to get my mind right for this season—football season. It started in the training room, then the weight room, then gradually to the practice field.

In other words, I had to earn it.

I had to decide if I was going to make this a season to remember for all the right reasons.

CHAPTER 10

Who Do People Say We Are?

Preseason Camp

In Mark 8:27–29, as Jesus and His disciples were walking to the villages of Caesarea Philippi, He asked them, "Who do people say that I am?" They answered, "John the Baptist; others, Elijah; still others, one of the prophets."

"'But you,'" He asked them, 'who do you say that I am?'"

When I was reading this passage during the summer of 2011, while strengthening and conditioning for the fall after such an upside-down spring, I immediately thought of our football team. The disciples were with Jesus all the time. He heard everything they heard. He knew what people had to say about Him and what they called Him. The difference was that He didn't pay attention to what other people said. Jesus came to this world to accomplish one thing, and that's all He was focused on. He knew His own identity, so it didn't really matter what people said about Him; He was just focused on His work.

The same is true for a football team. Every team has an identity. The fans, the media, and other teams each have their own ideas of what that identity is. For us at Alabama, they would always talk us up as being something more than we were, saying how unstoppable we were, that we were easily on our way to another title. But just like Jesus, we couldn't listen to any of that outside noise. We needed to remain focused on our identity.

And a team's identity is established during preseason camp.

One time I was talking with one of our big-time signees, and I asked him why he chose Alabama. He told me he visited Florida, Auburn, Georgia, and Mississippi State. All of them talked about beating Alabama and how that was their biggest game of the year. He thought, *Why don't I just go to Alabama where I can play in a big game every week?* He's right. Everybody has an opinion about Alabama football.

But you can't focus on what others say about you. You can't worry about the target on your back. You can't focus on what the other team does. You can only focus on being the best player you can be.

Coach Saban made sure we never forgot that.

On the Fridays before every game, he always told us the upcoming game would be determined by what *we* do, not how good the other team was or their game plan. It would come down to how well we executed and the discipline we demonstrated on the field. He never talked to us about winning or losing. I honestly don't think that was ever his goal or his intention for us. All he wanted was for us to be the best people and the best football players we could be. That's why during preseason camp, the only thing we worked on were our fundamentals, becoming masters at our positions, learning every single detail about what it took to do our jobs.

On our first day of camp to open the 2011 season, Coach got all of us together in a meeting and asked what we wanted our team to accomplish. As he looked around the room, we thought about it. "These are things you think about for the rest of your life," he said.

Without a doubt, we knew we could win it all in 2011. We were capable of winning it in 2010, but we didn't do the little things right. We had all the talent with Mark, Julio, Marcell, and so on, but we didn't do our due diligence. We ended up beating ourselves.

Everyone has their opinions for why we lost those three games that year, but I believe it started in camp. We couldn't let that happen in 2011. We had given ourselves a wonderful opportunity, and we had all the potential in the world to fulfill our opportunity. Our potential was limitless.

At the same time, though, potential means nothing. All great things come only from sacrifice, not potential. Everything in the world has a price, and the price is sacrifice. I love Hebrews 12:11: "No discipline seems enjoyable at the time, but painful. Later on, however, it yields the fruit of peace and righteousness to those who have been trained by it."

You either suffer the pain of discipline or the pain of disappointment.

Camp is when a team must decide which route to take. Camp is where everyone buys into the team and sets their personal agendas aside so they can do what's best for the whole. A poster outside our locker room said it all: "Out of yourself, into the team." That's what football's all about. That's what *life* is all about.

Personally, camp was a great time for me to reflect. During this time of year, everyone moved into Bryant Hall, and we all lived there until right before classes started. All my time was spent with my teammates. And this year, after everything that had happened with the tornado and all, I really needed that. I needed *them*. They were my brothers, and I will always appreciate how they took me in and made sure I was OK. I never let anyone treat me any different, nor did I ever let them feel sorry for me. I told them to make fun of me when I did something stupid, just like they'd always done before. But my teammates really expedited my healing process.

Going into camp, I was probably about 85 percent of where I needed to be in terms of being able to play. I was a little bit stiff and still had a slight limp when I ran. But I competed against myself every day to close that gap. I wanted to be 100 percent—the best I could be at what God had given me the ability to do.

The only thing on my mind was football. No "mental clutter," as Coach Saban calls it. I only brought a few things into the dorm with me: some toiletries, a few snacks, a change of clothes, and my Bible, which I read every night. And one of the verses I remember reading was Hebrews 12:1—"Let us run with endurance the race that lies before us."

That kind of said it all. God had set out a race for me. The 2011 season—as hard as it had become before it even started—was my race. And I was being called to run it. With endurance.

I knew my team would be running it right along with me.

After a tough camp in always sweltering Tuscaloosa, we were ready for our first game week. With nineteen starters and fifty-one lettermen returning, we couldn't help but be optimistic. Back was the bulk of our offensive line—Barrett Jones, William Vlachos, Chance Warmack, and D. J. Fluker. Darius Hanks and Marquis Maze, along with tight end Michael Williams, were solid in their receiving positions. The combination of Trent Richardson (poised to step into Mark Ingram's shoes) and Eddie Lacy was a great one-two punch for us in the backfield.

Defensively, Mark Barron, Dont'a Hightower, Courtney Upshaw, Dre Kirkpatrick, DeQuan Menzie, Dee Milliner, Robert Lester, Nico Johnson, Josh Chapman, Damion Square, and C. J. Mosley—along with juco transfers Jesse Williams and Quinton Dial—promised to be a salty bunch that would be tough for anyone to score on.

And of course, all the specialists were back—me as the long snapper, Cody Mandell as the punter, and Jeremy Shelley and Cade Foster as the placekickers (Jeremy primarily for short-yardage kicks, Cade for the long ones).

But again, no matter the talent, or the fan's expectations, or the media's predictions, it would all come down to an identity, an identity no one but the players could forge. In Coach Saban's first big press conference to open up fall camp, I couldn't help but take notice of his words:

> We are excited about the challenges and opportunities this team has this year. By every indication that we've seen in the first couple of practices, we have a lot of guys that are committed to a high standard. We obviously, like every team, have some question marks and challenges. Some players on the team need to take advantage of those opportunities created by those questions and challenges, and how that all works out

will go a long way in determining where this team can go. It's not really about expectations. It's really about how many guys go and do their job on a consistent basis versus how many blinking lights we have of guys who don't seem to be able to get it right, whether it's personally, academically, or athletically. All of those things contribute to the competitive character and consistency that you can go out and play with.

Who did people say we were? We were about to find out.

CHAPTER 11

Setting a Standard

Kent State • September 3, 2011 • Tuscaloosa

One of the most inspiring things to see in Tuscaloosa after the tornado was people rebuilding. Rebuilding their houses, schools, businesses, churches, everything. It always gave me chill bumps to see people bringing back to life what was lost or to see a sign that said, "We're coming back." I especially loved the ones that read, "T-Town, Never Down."

During the two years following the tornado, I helped Habitat for Humanity in building a couple of houses. Each of those homes, like every good house, started with a foundation and a structured frame. Our football team was built the same way, but we had a different name for it—a "standard"—just as Coach mentioned in his precamp press conference. At the end of the day, the standard we set for ourselves and for the team would be the most important thing. And if we or the leadership weren't setting a standard for the team, then who *would* be? That's easy—someone who *shouldn't* be.

Discipline, character, hard work, toughness, commitment, effort, and pride are all things that comprise a team's standard. And none of these happen by accident. Coach Saban and the leadership on the team are what made it happen. All these things were instilled in us from the day we arrived on campus. Every year Coach would tell the new freshman class, "Before we win any kind of championship, we have to be a team full of champions." That is true in anything.

After the storm I set a standard for my life, and I committed to that standard. In Jesus' parable of the sower in Luke 8, He talks of four different destinations for a farmer's seed, which represents the Word of God. The first seed falls on a beaten path and gets trampled on and taken away by birds. Other seed falls on the rocks, but the plants that spring up wither and die. Some seed grows among the thorns but is eventually choked. Finally, good soil—rich in nutrients—awaits some of the seed, and a great crop is produced.

Jesus went on to explain this parable and what each soil represents. But the last kind of soil—the one that represents being rooted in the Word of God—is the standard I strive for. It's about holding fast to the Word and not being taken away by the birds or blown away by the wind. The Word became my standard.

And that standard naturally leads to certain commitments.

One of the toughest things for me after the tornado, for example, was telling myself I would not complain. I knew if I complained, I couldn't see the positive things that were going on around me. I made that a part of my standard.

For some reason, people would always come up to me and complain about the smallest things—"Why don't you think the city is doing this?" or "The insurance company only gave me 'x' amount of dollars," and so forth. People would find the silliest stuff to complain about and just vent to me and expect me to complain along with them so they would feel better about themselves. I always told myself, "Don't complain, don't complain." Sometimes I would just have to walk away from them.

I know that sounds rude, but I stayed committed to my standard. Because once you compromise your standard, no matter how small, it gets easier and easier to do. I knew God had set an agenda for me—to reflect His Word, to be positive, to be a blessing, to carry myself as the person He had made me to be—and if I was living someone else's agenda or by someone else's standard, I couldn't fulfill mine. Just as everyone has a role on the team—the quarterback can't play offensive line, the running back can't play safety, the long snapper can't kick—everyone must do his job in order for the team to be successful.

And my job was to be myself, to live my standard.

On the Sunday night before the home opener, the University held a campus candlelight vigil at Palmer Lake to honor Ashley and the other UA students who had died in the storm, as well as all the students, faculty, and staff who had participated in the rebuilding process. UA President Robert Witt summed up what I had witnessed all summer by saying that although the tornado had been the worst tragedy in school history, "It will also go down as one of the finest moments in our University's history."

Coach Saban, in his remarks, told everyone Dr. B's "Earn it" story from *Saving Private Ryan*. I wondered how Coach knew the story until I found out that Dr. B had sent it to him in an e-mail. Coach also challenged everyone to follow the model of Jesus Christ and serve others.

I know folks left there saying, "Wow."

The first game of 2011 against Kent State was huge for me. I had worked hard all summer with this one date in mind—September 3—and now that day was finally here. Everyone in the community was highly anticipating this game as well. It had been a long few months leading up to opening day. It was also the first time many people were able to see what Tuscaloosa actually looked like after the storm. It looked much different in person than on television or in photos.

There was a lot of buildup and hype around this game. We were playing Kent State, which is Coach Saban's alma mater. But despite the raw emotions surrounding the game, he still brought the team's focus back to one thing—football.

Everyone was talking about how this game would bring back a sense of "normalcy" around town. Coach Saban looked at all of us the day before the game and asked it a different way: What is normal for us? What is our standard?

We had won thirty-six games the past three seasons—that was normal for us. We had been in the SEC Championship Game twice in the past three years—that was normal for us. Coach said that everything we wanted to accomplish started right now. We didn't have the season we wanted the year before, and now was the time for us to change it. He asked us what our team's identity would be. He said we'd establish it right here in this first game. All we needed to do was play to our standard.

That's how every game was for Coach. Our goal as players was to win every game, yet all he wanted was for us to be the best players we could be. Never look at the scoreboard.

Everything else will take care of itself. Stay focused on the process.

Play to the standard.

After hearing Coach talk on Friday, I couldn't have been more ready to get out there. After our specialists meeting, I looked around at my teammates, guys who had been with me through it all—a group that had really bonded over the past few months—and told them how much I loved them and how much I appreciated everything they had done for me. I told them about how everything we do comes down to us; it's all on our shoulders. We'd already made all the kicks in practice; we'd put in all the work. Now it was time to collect, to follow through on it. I told them we were starting our campaign right now to be the best specialists in the country.

I couldn't wait.

After a good night's rest at the team hotel, I woke up Saturday morning ready to play. We had an early 11:20 a.m. kickoff on the SEC Network, so by 6:00 we were up for our customary game-day routine—a choice of two chapel services (one Catholic and one nondenominational), our pregame meal, and then back to the room, where Jeremy and I just chilled out and watched *GameDay* on ESPN. Then we loaded the buses and took the short ride down University Boulevard to Bryant-Denny Stadium.

Even with the early kickoff, thousands of Alabama fans welcomed us at the Walk of Champions, a large plaza that recognizes our five national champion coaches and all our SEC and national championship teams. Looking at the fans, especially the kids, I couldn't help but think back to being right there many years earlier, yelling and screaming for my Crimson Tide.

I had made this walk many times, but on this day things were different. I quickly realized we weren't the only ones ready for a game—so were the fans. They, too, had experienced the tornado and its aftermath. They, too, were starving for something to take their minds off the life-changing moments of 129 days earlier. They, too, needed a dose of hearing the PA announcer say, "THIS is Alabama Football!"

And at the end of the Walk of Champions, as we made a left turn toward our locker room, there they stood—my parents—right on cue, underneath the statues of the two football players symbolizing the year 1892, the first year of Crimson Tide football. At every game during my five years at Alabama, they never missed being at that spot to give me a hug and a word of encouragement.

Not one of those pregame walks went by that I didn't think back ten or twelve years earlier, remembering how despite their weakness and sickness from their individual bouts with cancer, they always made sure they were there for me—never failing to attend a ball game of mine, never leaving me without life's necessities, never allowing me to miss out on being a normal kid. After all I had gone through just a few months earlier, I knew my playing in this first game was as meaningful for them as it was for me, perhaps even more.

After getting taped and dressed, the specialists were ready to go out. As we huddled up right before running out of the tunnel, I looked them all in the eye and said, "Look around, guys, it's just us here, no one else. Look at us, we did it. Don't let anyone ever tell you that you can't do something. Remember this moment right now for the rest of your life. I love y'all." Then I broke it down on, "Ch, Ch," and everyone else went "BOOOOMM" and we sprinted out onto the field.

I was so excited, screaming like a little kid. Since it was only around 10:00 in the morning and the game didn't start until 11:30 or so, there was hardly anyone in the stands.

But despite the near empty stadium, I felt a serene sense of accomplishment in that moment. I had overcome adversity. I had gone through one of the toughest things I'll hopefully ever face in my life, and I had come out on top. I still had a lot to go through, both with my body and as a football player, but in that moment I was a winner.

———————

Bryant-Denny Stadium never looked better than it did that day, a welcome sight for the sellout crowd of almost 102,000. Huge houndstooth ribbons adorned the field. In pregame ceremonies, our governor, Dr. Robert Bentley, honored the tornado's first responders who had put their lives on the line to save others.

Before the game, the Kent State players—several of whom had been in Tuscaloosa earlier in the summer helping build a Habitat house—were looking around in awe of the stadium and the number of fans we had in there.

For me, that day wasn't about our 48–7 victory over Kent State; it was more about a victory of another sorts.

I had won a battle, but God was not finished with me.

Or with any of us.

CHAPTER 12

Energy Source

Penn State • September 10, 2011 • State College, Pennsylvania

Coach Saban's undergrad degree is in business, but it might as well have been in sports psychology. He's a master at picking up on the smallest things around practice and meetings—things that no one else would ever consider relevant to winning football games—and going crazy about them.

One of the things he would harp on was the energy of the players in meetings. He hated to see negative energy in meetings—people yawning, resting their heads on their hands, not paying attention. Coach would always say he could tell what kind of practice we were going to have just by the energy we exhibited in meetings. The right attitude, he said, always comes before success.

If we affected the team with our negative energy, we were being a traitor to the team.

Bill Belichick, head coach of the New England Patriots and a great friend of Coach Saban's, once talked about how energy during a game can have an effect on the outcome.

In the NFL Films documentary *A Football Life*, Belichick recalled a time when his team made an interception during a playoff road game, but the players on the sideline didn't show a lot of excitement about it, didn't bring any energy to the moment. They ended up losing the game. Their lack of energy had borne an impact on the outcome.

The next year, however, the same thing happened—an interception on the road during a key playoff game—only this time the team brought so much positive energy, jumping up, high-fiving, congratulating each other, it changed the entire momentum of the game. This time the Patriots won. Belichick said the only difference was the energy after that interception.

During Penn State week, Coach Saban made a huge emphasis on our energy, not only during practice but also on the sideline during the game. This game would come down to us and the energy we brought to the field, he said. It wouldn't be about their players, their fans, or their stadium. It would be about us, just as it always is.

And key to that energy would be the energy of our leadership.

Leaders must inspire everyone else and make sure they have the energy and mind-set to do their job. From everything I've learned from Coach Saban, I believe that's the No. 1 job and trademark of a leader: getting others to do their job or to do it better.

Throughout my career, I took that message to heart. I mean, look, I'm a long snapper. I wasn't on the field seventy plays like a lot of the starters. I usually played only about twelve to fifteen plays per game. So as a leader on the team, I needed to find my niche.

Coach brings in people to do leadership tests to figure out what your strengths and weaknesses are, and I found out from the results of those tests that one of my strengths is charisma. I'd always heard that word and I thought I knew what it meant, but I looked it up anyway and found the exact meaning:

Charisma: compelling attractiveness or charm that can inspire devotion in others.

I learned that I could affect others with my positive energy. I couldn't get onto the linebackers when they missed a tackle like Dont'a Hightower could or call out the offensive linemen when they missed a block like Trent Richardson could. I couldn't get in front of the whole team and give a pregame speech like A. J. McCarron could. But I could affect others with my energy, and I worked hard to develop that. One by one, I made sure I talked to everyone on the team just to give them some encouragement, make them laugh, or help them in some way. My job was to be an energy source. And through it all, I got to develop great relationships with all of my teammates.

In Exodus 17, Moses and the Israelites were fighting the Amalekites. As long as Moses held his staff above his head, the Israelites were winning. Every time Moses got tired, however, his staff began to lower and they started losing. Aaron and Hur then sat Moses down on a rock and helped him hold up his staff by propping up his arms with their hands. Because of this action, the Israelites won the war. That's what I wanted to do—lift people up.

Not only did I want to be a leader on my team, but I also wanted to be a leader in the community. I didn't know exactly how or what I could do, so I just decided I would do the same things I had done on the football team—try to affect people with my positive energy. Every time I was interviewed, I always said something uplifting about what was happening either in my life or in the community. My idea was that if people thought I was sitting around feeling bad for myself and then saw how positive I was on television or in the paper, they would look at their own obstacles differently too. I wanted to have a positive impact on everyone with whom I came in contact.

Attitudes are contagious, especially negative attitudes. So I tried never to hang out with negative people. I didn't want them to impact me. I always tried to surround myself with positive people—the people I called "my team." I'm not talking about my football team (although I had them too) but a small group of people I always kept with me. I had my family, who are always there for me, as well as a few others, including my old roommate, Payton Holley.

Payton went through the same thing I went through with the tornado, and he kept a positive attitude just as I did. It's hard to stay positive all the time, but we made each other do it. We would talk to each other about everything. We had a vision for each other, and we kept helping each other maintain it. One of my favorite quotes is from former Baltimore Ravens linebacker Ray Lewis: "It's hard to stop a man with a vision, but you *cannot* stop a *team* with a vision." I believe the only way you can have a true impact on someone's life is if you share common ground with them, if you have a relationship with them. Tuscaloosa residents didn't know me personally, but we all went through very similar difficulties. So when I'd go out and speak in the community, I could have an impact on them because we had a relationship, and at the same time they could have an impact on me.

I've made this my motto since the storm: "People ask for blessings, but I ask God that I can be a blessing." That's why we're here, you and me. God has put you in a certain spot in your life, and I believe He put you there so you can be a blessing to the people with whom you have relationships and common ground. Being a blessing to others creates the positive energy to make a difference in someone's life.

Allow me to give you a real-life example of energy in action. For my project management class in school, our group assignment was to build and facilitate the construction of a Habitat for Humanity house. We did the fund-raising and coordinated the volunteers for the entire project. I learned so much from this undertaking, both for school and for my life. But one of the most important lessons I learned was about being a blessing.

In a project called "Get Jackie Home for Christmas," our class, along with Calvary Baptist Church, built a house for Jackie Wright, best known as "Ms. Jackie," on the west side of Tuscaloosa. Ms. Jackie worked at DCH Regional Medical Center for more than twenty-five years, but all of her money had gone to support her kids, her family, and other people in her community. She was a blessing to them and everyone knew it. She brought so much positive energy to all the people around her.

We made a video to promote what we were doing, in which we interviewed several of her neighbors, and all of them spoke of their love for Ms. Jackie. Even before we asked, they each recalled a time when she had been so helpful to them.

Ms. Jackie gave me a tour of her old house. The walls had holes and leaks in them, it cost a fortune to keep the place at a comfortable temperature, and she didn't have hot water. There's no way anyone could have lived there comfortably, but Ms. Jackie never complained. She just helped others.

So we raised the money and built her a brand-new house. And when we dedicated it, she talked about how she had always prayed to be a blessing to other people. On this day, though, everyone who helped build that house was a blessing to her.

You never know what your positive attitude and energy will inspire in those around you.

––––––––––

Going in to play the storied Penn State Nittany Lions, our mission was clear—to use our positive energy to make a difference. They had declared this game one of their "Whiteouts," where all the home fans in their 110,000-seat stadium wear white to energize the crowd and create a very hostile environment for the visiting team. Coach Saban told us that the whiteout would only make a difference if we thought it would, but as long as we did what we came to do, it wouldn't matter. Again before the game, he talked about how our energy on the sideline would make a huge difference.

In our specialists' meeting on the Thursday before the game, I had told our placekicker Cade Foster a story about a greeting they share in Zimbabwe. In their language, one says to another, "Are you strong?" And the response to that is, "I'm strong if you're strong." It means, "If you're ready to go, then I'm ready to go." I knew it would be a hostile environment in State College, and we would need to be prepared for anything. But I told the specialists that our performance would come down to us, to this core group of teammates. All we had was each other. It wasn't about the jerseys or the stadium or the fans. It came down to us. We would get our power—our strength—from each other.

Coming out of the tunnel for pregame warm-ups, the sight of Beaver Stadium took my breath away. All you could see was white except for the few thousand Alabama fans proudly displaying their crimson. Even the white goalposts blended into the crowd, making them difficult for our place-kickers to see.

Things were tense during warm-ups. My heart was beating so hard I could feel my shoulder pads moving. But I knew I had to keep my cool. I couldn't let the younger guys see that side of me, especially Cade. He was counting on me. He then just looked at me and said, "Are you strong?" Just hearing him say that put me immediately at ease. With a smile I said, "I'm strong if you're strong." Cade was ready to go, and that made me ready to go.

After spotting Penn State an early field goal, we scored twenty-seven straight points before they scored a touchdown and two-point conversion in the last two minutes.

I must say our energy on the field—and the sideline— was off the charts, even early in the game when we were behind. We definitely took to heart Coach's challenge to provide positive energy to each other. And as our energy increased, the Penn State crowd's energy decreased, although I do have to commend their students for staying until the end. (Afterward we learned that the crowd was the largest ever to see a Crimson Tide team play, which we thought was cool.)

A. J. McCarron's performance that day—19 of 31 for 163 yards and a rope touchdown pass to Michael Williams—earned him the starting quarterback nod and launched his career toward becoming Alabama's all-time leading passer.

Truly, the lessons we learned that day on the importance of energy would prepare us for bigger and better things down the road.

CHAPTER 13

The Little Things

North Texas • September 17, 2011 • Tuscaloosa

We had just come off a great win over Penn State in front of all their "whited-out" fans. It was an awesome feeling, but this week we had North Texas. People said this would be an easy game, that we could let off the gas a little bit, that we didn't have much to worry about. Stuff like that.

But not our coaches, not Coach Saban.

Every week, no matter who we were playing, it was the biggest game of the year because, as Coach always said, "If you don't win this one, the next one isn't that important anymore." It came down to who we were and what we wanted to accomplish. If we wanted to be the best team and the best players, why should it matter who we were playing? If we were planning on playing the best game of our lives, it shouldn't matter who we were playing against.

Coach would always say that's why Michael Jordan was the best and was so dominant, because he never played down to his competition. He always played his game and wasn't affected by anything else, not the opponent or the crowd, nothing. He always played to his standard.

Our football team was made up of the little things like this. Whether it was taking off our cleats after practice before we came into the locker room, or tucking our shirt in during a workout so everyone was in uniform, it was always the little things. Even in the games, defensive end Damion Square would always say, "This game is going to come down to four or five plays, and you never know which plays they're going to be, so you have to give everything you have on every single play."

Stack up all the little things, and that's where great things come from. Coach always told us that paying attention to detail would earn us tremendous results.

But it's so hard to focus on the little things, especially in practice.

After a long day of studying and classes, we would start meetings every day at 2:00, then practice around 4:00. Practice seemed monotonous to me early in my career, but I soon learned that practice was the reason we were so good. All we worked on in practice were the little things, developing good habits.

And when it's all said and done, the majority of what we do is a direct result of the habits we've created for ourselves. Coach Saban instilled in each of us the habits of being a good football player.

After I started to realize this, I actually began to enjoy practice. I enjoyed the drills and the work I was putting in. I realized it was making me a great long snapper. I would go out and compete against myself every day, forcing myself to get better. I learned that you don't stay the same—you either get better or you get worse. And if you think you're staying the same, you're probably getting worse. I focused on the little things as a snapper and worked toward getting a little bit better every day.

I also noticed that I could change the slightest thing in my technique and get tremendous results. If I wasn't getting the spiral I needed on my snaps, I would just move my left thumb down maybe a half centimeter, and when I snapped the ball it would have a tight spiral as it zipped back there. I talked to Jeremy about his placekicking, and he said the same thing: he would make the smallest adjustments to how he kicked, and the ball would come out straighter and have much more consistency.

Little things. They make a huge difference.

———————

I mentioned earlier that both of my parents had cancer when I was young. My mom had ovarian cancer when I was in the third grade, and my dad had melanoma when I was in the seventh grade. Even though I was young, I still took away so many lessons from those experiences and learned so much from my parents' example. I learned all about the little things from both of them. They made sure they did all of the little things right. They couldn't control the big things like their cancer, but they could control making sure I knew they loved me.

"How you do anything is how you do everything"— that's one of my favorite quotes I picked up from Coach Cochran, and it all goes back to doing the little things right. The kids that usually don't do things right when it comes to football are the same ones who are late to class, miss study hall, and are sloppy in their habits. Coach Saban always talked about how doing the little things is not a switch you can just turn on whenever you want. It's an all-the-time thing, not just a sometimes thing.

While I was at Alabama, I learned that my success, the team's success, any success, came down to the little things and how much effort I gave all the time. I usually broke it down to one day at a time. Some days I had to break it down to one meal at a time. I never tried to focus on the big picture all at once.

Long-time defensive coordinator Monte Kiffin, who coached at Tennessee during the 2009 season, would always say, "See a little, see a lot. See a lot, see nothing." When I was recovering from the tornado, I couldn't look at my recovery through the big-picture lens. I needed to take everything one step at a time and focus on the little things. I needed to get just a little bit better every day. It was (as if you haven't seen this word enough) a process. It can't be anything else. When I started my rehab, if I had tried to get better all in one day, I would obviously have failed and never started again.

It always comes back to the little things.

In the North Texas game, we emphasized the little things just as much as if we'd been playing LSU or Auburn or Tennessee, and we played one of our best overall games in the 41–0 victory. We held North Texas to under a hundred yards, while our offense totaled 586 total yards, including Trent Richardson's 167 yards on the ground and Eddie Lacy's 161 yards. Both were career highs for those guys, and in doing so, they became the first duo in Alabama history to rush for more than 150 yards in the same game.

With Kent State, Penn State, and North Texas in the history books, we turned our attention to the SEC schedule, which would comprise eight of our next nine games.

As far as we were concerned, a completely new season was beginning.

CHAPTER 14

The Why

Arkansas • September 24, 2011 • Tuscaloosa

Why do you do what you do?

Do you have a passion for it? If you have a passion for something and are committed to seeing your vision come true, you'll be willing to do whatever it takes to make it happen. And when you start to struggle, you'll dig down deep and think about why you want it so bad.

It's called the *Why*. For some people, it's their kids. For others, it's their friends. For some, it's a cause or a mission.

For linebacker Nico Johnson, it was his mom.

Nico came in and got a lot of playing time as a freshman in 2009. He contributed significantly to the championship team that year and had high hopes of playing a lot more in 2010. But in May 2010, Nico's mom lost her battle with diabetes.

Nico's mom became his *why*. You could see it all during the off-season. He'd be running 110s all summer, and tears would be running down his face. You could see his passion; you knew why he was out there. He knew why he was there, to make his mom proud. That's all he was thinking about.

I asked Nico about it, and he told me that when he thought he was tired, he could hear his mom telling him how proud she was of him. So he ran and he ran in her memory, unlike I've ever seen anyone do before. He came in first every single time, even while he was crying. And in 2010, he had one of his best seasons.

Everyone knew about Nico and what had happened.

We all knew his *why*.

People compliment Coach Saban about how his teams actually *play* like a team, how it's obvious on the field they're looking out for each other. I believe one of the reasons is because they know why everyone is out there.

We knew everyone's *why*—whether it was Nico's mom, or Coach Cochran's kids, or the fact that someone's teacher once told him he'd never amount to anything and would never play in the NFL (a guy who later became a first-round pick). We knew what everyone wanted to do and why they were there. And if someone wasn't holding on to their part and doing their job, they could count on another player to come along and remind them why they were out there. We all knew everyone's *whys*.

It was obvious what mine was. It was dated April 27. But it was actually even more than that. In my mind, I was playing for anyone who had ever lost something or who thought they couldn't do something they had once dreamed of doing. I was playing for the people who were going through adversity, no matter what it was, but who needed the heart and courage to win their battle.

Tuscaloosa—the community I had fallen in love with the previous three years—was my *why*. When I thought I couldn't go another step, I thought about all the students who passed away, including Ashley. I thought about how blessed

I was, including the blessing of being able to give back. I was committed to making the best of it.

I came into the 2011 season with so much passion. It was just different that year. It was about so much more than football. Coming through what I'd endured since the tornado, it really wasn't hard to know my *why* and to stay focused on what I needed to do.

But what about when it's *not* easy to be passionate about something? That's where passion becomes a real choice, where you refuse just to go through the motions, where you "strain your gut," as Coach Cochran used to yell at us in practice. You lock on to your *why*, and you let it drive your forward momentum and effort. With a passion.

———

We knew Arkansas was going to be tough. They had a great quarterback in Tyler Wilson and a much-improved defense. Coach really emphasized that we needed to win our battles—including the special teams battle.

For about two years, we had been practicing a fake field goal called "ARMY" and Coach Saban told us all week we needed to be ready to run it. So when our opening drive stalled on the Arkansas 37-yard line, he huddled up the field goal unit on the sideline. Everyone was dead silent, but we all knew what we wanted to hear: "ARMY."

He was probably thinking of a thousand different scenarios that could happen in terms of field position and risk/reward. It was like he was in a chess match with the opposing coach. I always loved seeing that look on his face. He glanced up at the scoreboard, then out on the field, then back at us a couple of times, then finally said, "All right, run ARMY."

We ran out the same way as always and lined up in field goal formation for a 54-yarder. Then A. J., the regular holder, yelled, "ARMY, ARMY SHIFT," and Cade Foster split out to the left with our tight end Chris Underwood. Then A. J. stood up in shotgun formation, sending Chris in motion to the right. I snapped to A. J. and the receivers flooded the right side of the field, while Michael Williams, who was lined up on the right, came back behind the line and ran down the left sideline.

I was supposed to pass block with the rest of the offensive line, but no one was rushing through me, so I literally just stood there because I didn't want to get called for an illegal man downfield. I looked down and saw Michael wide open. I saw the football fly over my head and watched him catch it for the touchdown. The home crowd went crazy.

I sprinted down the field as fast as I could. It was actually the only time I'd ever been able to celebrate in the end zone after being part of a touchdown play, so I was determined to make the most of it. I chest-bumped Michael and ran in front of the student section trying to pump them up. I probably looked ridiculous, but it felt so good and was so much fun. When I retook the field to snap the extra point afterwards, I was seriously out of breath, but it was a good snap and a good kick. We continued to celebrate all the way to the sideline.

Special teams played a huge role in that game. In addition to the fake field goal, Marquis Maze weaved in and out of what looked like the whole Arkansas punt team on his way to an 83-yard punt return, the tenth longest in school history. I had to do a double-take to be sure it wasn't Javier Arenas out there, back in an Alabama uniform.

So despite what should ordinarily have been a close contest, we ran away with a 38–14 win. We knew our team was capable of rising to any challenge. More important, we knew *why* we were doing it.

And within just a few hours, all attention would turn to Florida and a trip to the Swamp.

CHAPTER 15

Power from Within

Florida • October 1, 2011 • Gainesville, Florida

The Swamp in Gainesville, Florida, is without a doubt the most hostile environment in which I have ever played a football game. Their student section is directly behind the visiting team's bench, and they scream in your ears from the moment you step on the playing surface. Before the game, a Florida student was arrested for running around on the field. I remember thinking, *This place is absolutely crazy.*

Florida won the toss and chose to receive. On the first play of the game, they threw a fly route down the sideline—just over the head of Dre Kirkpatrick—for a 65-yard score. The stadium erupted. Fans were screaming and jumping and throwing their cups and drinks in the air. The place was pure bedlam. Before our offense had even played a down, Florida led 7–0.

We never had any doubt, though. Coach Saban always talks about how much time and energy he invests in the mental side of football, and it pays off in situations like these.

It all comes down to: What are you telling yourself? At Alabama we call it self-talk, or "I said to myself . . ."

It's basically this—the situation you're in is not what causes how you feel; the way you feel is determined by what you're telling yourself. During workouts or before practice, Coach Cochran was almost certain to tell us at some point to "calculate an attitude"—to make up our mind beforehand what kind of practice we were going to have. Success comes from having the right mind-set. The right attitude always comes first.

When I first learned about this at Alabama through programs like *PX2* and motivational speakers such as Trevor Moawad and Kevin Elko, I thought it was some kind of new science thing no one had ever really heard of. But the more I read my Bible, I learned that people have been doing this for a long time.

Jesus' disciple Thomas, for example—commonly referred to as "Doubting Thomas" because of his initial skepticism about Jesus rising from the dead—actually is known by two names in the Bible, one of which is Didymus, meaning "the twin." I assumed he really was a twin, but because of what we know about him, this "twin" reference makes me realize there's a lot of Thomas in all of us. We each have two sides—a believing side and a doubting side—and our believing side must encourage the doubting side through some healthy doses of self-talk.

First Samuel 30 tells the story of when David and his troops returned from war, only to discover that their wives and kids had been captured and their houses burned down. All the men wanted to stone David—kill him—but the Bible says he "found strength in the LORD his God" (v. 6). David drew his strength and power from within.

When the tornado came through Tuscaloosa, it knocked down just about every power line in town. I don't think anyone in the city had power, even the hospital. But the hospital had generators; they manufactured their power from within.

That's how our 2011 team was. Our power came from inside. That's how every individual on the team was wired. So when Florida threw that touchdown pass on the first play and the stadium erupted, we knew the game was still up to us. It wouldn't be defined by that one play. It would be defined by how we responded.

So in a vicious environment where we could hardly hear ourselves think, we calmly, methodically drove down the field to the 14-yard line on our first offensive series. After stalling there, Coach sent in the field goal unit. I remember looking at Jeremy and saying, "All right man, let's do this."

I had a routine I went through before all of my snaps, and I always talked to myself while doing it. I would line up, put my hands on the ball, and say to myself: "Trust." That completely cleared my mind. It reminded me that my body knew how to snap better than my brain did; I just needed to quit thinking and let my body takeover. Without hesitation, I snapped the ball to A. J., and Jeremy knocked home the 32-yard field goal.

The Gators matched the field goal a few minutes later, but after that it was all Alabama. Watching Trent Richardson bulldoze through the Florida defenders, piling up career highs in rushing yards (181) and carries (29), was a thing of beauty. Our defense, led by linebacker Courtney Upshaw, held the Gators to just 15 yards rushing.

In his postgame remarks, Coach Saban used a boxing analogy to describe our victory.

> In boxing, you never know when you
> have a good fighter until the guy gets hit,

gets staggered, and you see how he takes a punch. I think one of the most important things in this game is when things didn't go well early, especially defensively, there was really no panic. In a tough environment, in a tough situation, I was really pleased with the way our team sort of competed through a lot of things that happened early.

In other words, we found our power from within.

CHAPTER 16

Choices

Vanderbilt • October 8, 2011 • Tuscaloosa

We were now 5–0 and playing pretty well—not our best but pretty good football. On the Monday of Vanderbilt week, Coach Saban asked all of us, "Where do you want to go from here? How do you want to be remembered? How much does this season mean to you? It's all about the choices you make from here."

We were the fourth Alabama team in a row to have a perfect record after five games. In 2008 and 2009, both of those teams stayed focused on the process and finished the regular season undefeated. And of course, our 2009 squad went on to win the BCS championship. (I'll discuss the "Process" in the next chapter.)

The 2010 team, however, drifted away from the process. We began to focus just on winning ball games rather than focusing on what it takes to win. Everyone wants to win the game on Saturday, but that's not as important as how you prepare and what you choose to focus on during the week. It's all about the choices you make.

I've learned, both in football and in life, the main factors in success are the choices you make—what you choose to concentrate on, what you choose to spend your time on, the decisions you make about whether or not to do the right thing, the little things. Your decisions affect your future.

When I speak to middle school students, I often talk about how the choices and decisions they're making will directly impact their future and their life. I start by telling them they have freedom of choice but not freedom of consequence. If they'd rather sleep than do their homework, that's a choice they can make. But they can't decide what kind of consequences will result from it. That part's not up to them—or to any of us.

I tell them we only get twenty-four hours in a day. Everyone gets the same amount. The playing field is perfectly even, as far as our available time goes. But everyone chooses to spend their time differently. That's what separates people. If you were to write down your daily time schedule and what you did, it would say a lot about you. Where are you spending the majority of your time? Watching TV, or becoming a better person? Are you *spending* your life, or are you *investing* your life?

It's a choice you make.

If you'll sacrifice being lazy, you can choose to achieve your goals instead. If you'll sacrifice playing video games, you can choose to target your best effort on more important things. If you'll sacrifice sleeping in and eating whatever you want, you can choose to get up, to exercise, to be healthy, to hone your body into the best possible shape.

They're all choices.

When I was rehabbing, I made a choice: I was going to work hard, and I was going to get better. The first day I went to Champion Sports Medicine in Birmingham, I was in a wheelchair. Three months later, I finished my rehab in Tuscaloosa in football shape, all because I made a choice every day.

There's no other way.

———————

Choices were aplenty in the locker room at halftime of our game with Vanderbilt that year. I don't know whether we were still on an emotional high from the Arkansas and Florida wins, but for whatever reason, we came out flat and uninspired, despite a sold-out homecoming crowd. You'd think that by halftime, we'd have been up by three or four scores. But thanks to Vandy missing two field goals and giving up a last-second touchdown to us before the half, our lead was only 14–0. We didn't have the focus and discipline to make the right choices. And it showed.

In the locker room, Coach Saban was, let's say, quite persuasive with us. He talked about our inconsistency and lack of mental energy and intensity. He reminded us of the original questions he had asked us earlier in the week: "How do you want to be remembered? How much does this season mean to you?"

Well, we sure didn't want to be remembered as the Alabama team with such great expectations that lost to Vanderbilt.

Mentally, we made the right choices for the second half. Coach Saban made sure of that. Football-wise, we made the right adjustments on both sides of the ball. And after opening the second half with a 94-yard touchdown drive to go ahead 21–0, it was all Alabama from then on. The final 34–0 score was a direct result of some good, positive choices we all made at halftime.

Like I tell those middle schoolers, even today, it all comes back to choices. And the choices we made at halftime that afternoon kept us from facing the consequences.

CHAPTER 17

The Process

Ole Miss • October 15, 2011 •
Oxford, Mississippi

How do you respond when you have any sort of success? Do you just consider yourself accomplished and expect your success to naturally keep repeating itself? Or do you go back to the steps that made you successful to start with?

If there's anything I learned while I was at Alabama, it's that you don't rely on your success; you rely on what it took to get there.

Or, in Coach Saban-speak, the "Process."

Anybody who knows Coach Saban knows about the Process. That was his mantra when he first came to Alabama in 2007, and all the Alabama fans bought in quickly. They made T-shirts, bumper stickers, the whole nine yards. And yet most people who talk about the Process have no idea what it really is.

Everything we did at Alabama—practice, working out, off-season training, recruiting, how we ate, our academics, everything—it all had a process. Coach Saban had written down in detail what everyone was supposed to do and the reasons for doing it.

I remember when we'd plan the schedule for bowl practices or spring training. Coach would show us our schedules from the past three years, and even talk about how they did it at his previous schools and in the NFL. He would talk about how many days we should practice in a row, the times of the practices, how many hours we needed for rest and recovery.

The Process.

He never left out any detail, never left anything up to luck or chance. He always made sure he knew exactly what was going on and made sure we were prepared. He was so much on cue with the Process, in fact, that by my senior year I knew exactly what to expect. Going into meetings, I could usually tell most of the guys word for word what Coach was going to say.

Every time we had success, it was because we were focused on the Process. And every time we lost, it was because we *weren't* focused on the Process. We were focused more on the scoreboard, just winning, not on being a winner. The Process wasn't a magic formula. It was about discipline, pride, toughness, effort, all the things required to be successful in football—and in life.

Playing football at Alabama for me wasn't about the games we won, or the championship rings, or all the people I met. Sure, all of that stuff was an amazing experience. But when I think of my time at Alabama, I think of the person I became there. I think of all the principles that were instilled in me. I think about how many of the things I learned from Coach Saban and the Process relate directly to what I'm doing right now. I had seen how successful he had been at his chosen career and how he had given all the credit to his process of doing things. I can remember him saying, "I can't promise it'll work for you, but I can promise it won't work the other way."

I didn't know exactly as a college junior what I wanted to do with my life or what my future had in store, but I did want to be successful like Coach Saban. Not that I wanted money or fame, but I wanted to be as passionate about whatever I chose to do as he was. I wanted to be the best. I had never before seen success like Coach Saban's, but I knew I didn't want this to be the peak of my life. There are a lot of guys who have played at Alabama and tasted success, but when they finished playing, they didn't know where to go.

They veered away from the Process.

Jeremiah Castille, our team chaplain, is one of my favorite people. Every Saturday before our pregame meals, he would share the Word and always make biblical applications to football and the game we were playing that day. Jeremiah had played for Coach Bryant in the late '70s and early '80s, and he bought into Coach Bryant's process. He loves to say how he came to Alabama as an eighteen-year-old boy and left a twenty-two-year-old man. I feel the same way about my five years at Alabama. And if I stick with the Process, I know my growth curve is only going to head upward from here.

When we did all of the little things right as a team and stayed focused on the Process rather than being results oriented, we won, no matter what.

Just ask the Ole Miss Rebels.

The outmanned Rebs caught a taste of our Process that October afternoon, in the full-speed form of Trent Richardson and a stifling defense. Overshadowing our 52–7 win (including a 28-point third quarter) and Trent's 183 yards and 4 touchdowns was his 76-yard touchdown run when he twice juked an Ole Miss defensive back, the second move a jaw-dropping stop-and-go that left the guy frozen in his tracks.

After the game, we told Trent to give that guy his ankles back. It was simply that amazing. For days, Trent's run was the talk of the country. I bet it's received a million hits on YouTube.

Other than allowing an Ole Miss touchdown in the first three minutes of the game, we played about as well as we could. But despite our No. 2 ranking and our margins of victory to this point, we couldn't relax. We still needed to trust Coach Saban and the Process to get us ready—not just for down the road but for the next game.

For us, that meant Tennessee.

CHAPTER 18

Fighting Weary

Tennessee • October 22, 2011 • Tuscaloosa

By this time of the year—mid- to late-October—everyone is beat up. Everyone on every team has injuries, and you have to fight through them.

You have to fight weary.

That was a part of our identity at Alabama. That's what we were known for.

We would always compare our season to climbing a mountain. Coach Saban said that climbing a mountain never gets easier the higher you climb. The further up you go, the larger the obstacles and consequences become.

I played with some great athletes at Alabama, and it seemed like they were always playing with some kind of injury the entire time. Not huge ones—maybe a broken hand or a sprained ankle, something they could play with. Still, it would've been very easy and tempting to sit out a few games. And yet they played despite their injuries. That's what made them such great players.

Coach tried to get all of us to catch that philosophy and learn to play through our aches and pains. This went for mental fatigue too. Even though we had the best mental conditioning program in the country, there always came a time in the season when your brain needed a rest from football, sort of a second wind.

Fighting weary was especially important for this week's Tennessee game. It would have been very easy for us to look past it to the off week coming up, when we could rest and recover from a lot of our bangs and bruises. But Coach said, "Right now, everyone needs to be about right now." He talked about our 2009 team when, in anticipation of the off week, we overlooked Tennessee. In that game, we had our backs to the wall and needed to block two field goals—including one on the last play—to win the game.

Coach Saban always said, "If you're feeling tired and you can't find the energy to keep going, that's when you have to step back and remember the things you want to accomplish. That gives you the energy to keep going. If it matters as much to you as you say it does, you can keep fighting through it."

———————

Most of the time, practices are not fun. They're hot, they're long, and they push you to your physical and mental limits. But that's why Alabama is so good. That's why we were able to keep playing so hard in the fourth quarter. Getting that way, though, is not easy, especially in the last half of the season.

That's why everyone loved D. J. Fluker, our 6' 6", 335-pound man-beast.

D. J. brought so much energy to practice that, as a result, everyone loved practicing. It was still just as hard and taxing, but we learned to love it. D. J. would chant and scream, everyone would holler back at him, and then we'd all forget about the pain. We were having fun. We learned as a team how to enjoy practice, and that made us even better.

Thanks to guys like D. J., we quit looking at practice with such a negative vibe and instead began looking at it in a positive way. As a result, we saw that we were getting better. When anyone got tired, we just reminded them why we were out there—to be the best we could be.

Everyone gets tired and must learn how to fight weary and persevere. When I was doing my rehab and recovery, some days were harder than others, and some days I felt like I had lost. I didn't want to admit that, but looking back on it, that's what happened. I would get down, but I would never allow myself to stay down. If I had a day where I felt like I'd been whipped and wasn't going to make it, I would always wake up the next day with the attitude that God had awakened me for a chance to reload.

I think back to my parents and their battles with cancer. I've said this before, but if I hadn't seen the physical toll it took on them, I would never have known they had cancer. They had learned to fight weary.

Job 29:20 says, "My strength will be refreshed within me, and my bow will be renewed in my hand." This is one of those verses you can't really understand until you've experienced real difficulties in life. During rehab from my injuries, I would get tired, but I'd find the strength to persevere because I had a battle to fight.

Being weary is not what takes you out of the game. Only quitting does.

What'll it be for you?

During the week leading up to our game with Tennessee, we couldn't help but hear what had happened in Baton Rouge two weeks earlier. Near the end of the LSU-Florida game—a full four weeks before the "Game of the Century" between Alabama and LSU—Tiger fans had already started the "We want Bama!" chants.

In our preparations for Tennessee, the last thing in the world we wanted (or needed) to think about was the LSU game on November 5. Coach Saban preached all week not to listen to all the chatter and stay focused on Tennessee.

Well, the LSU hype must've gotten to us, because at halftime of the Tennessee game, we found ourselves deadlocked, 6–6. We had no mental intensity, energy, or focus. I suppose "lackluster" would be a good description. And so, similar to the way Coach chewed on us after our poor first half performance against Vanderbilt, he got hold of us again in the locker room during the Tennessee game. I mean a *good* hold of us.

And it must have worked because when we came back out, we were a different team. Thanks to A. J.'s pinpoint passing and some key defensive adjustments, we scored 31 second-half points and shut out Tennessee to win going away, 37–6.

Following the game, after my teammates had dressed and left, I welcomed Dr. B, my plastic surgeon, into the locker room. By this point of the season, I had done everything possible on my own in terms of treating my leg wound, and it still wasn't healing exactly right. The only procedure left was to do a skin graft.

Dr. B had done a ton of research and found this new procedure where you could get a skin graft from a cadaver. We figured this would be best so I wouldn't have to worry about two different wounds healing—one from the ankle and one from wherever he'd taken the skin. And because of the upcoming off week, we decided to do the procedure right after the Tennessee game so my ankle could rest and begin to heal properly.

Carrying around a cooler containing the skin mesh from the cadaver, Dr. B looked like a character right out of a movie. After sterilizing the training area in our locker room, he began the procedure, using his own instruments and using our student trainers as his staff. In about thirty minutes, I had someone else's skin on my leg.

We didn't take off the bandage until a full two weeks later, on the night before the LSU game. It was really cool to see skin over my leg for the first time since the tornado, even though it was a mesh. Of all the injuries I suffered because of the storm, my leg wound is the one that'll be a forever reminder of April 27, 2011. I can't thank Dr. B enough for the job he did in caring for me.

As we were walking off the field that night after the Tennessee win, echoes of "We want LSU" reverberated throughout Bryant-Denny Stadium. We knew the importance of this game and how excited our fans would be.

First, though, despite all the hype and distractions, we were determined to enjoy the off week.

CHAPTER 19

Lessons from Coach

Off Week

Every great coach has life lessons to offer. I've read books about Coach Bryant, John Wooden, Bobby Bowden, and so on, and all of those guys talk about life lessons. I was lucky enough to see this every day from the greatest coach I know, Nick Saban.

During the off week between the Tennessee and LSU games, Coach Saban turned sixty years old on October 31. That afternoon, when he walked into our team meeting room, we were all wearing birthday hats, blowing horns, and singing "Happy Birthday" like a bunch of four-year-olds. As a keepsake, we presented him a signed Alabama jersey with "SABAN" on the back and the number 60.

Coach got a big kick out of it. He looked at us and said: "Learn to appreciate this, guys. Don't take things like this for granted. When you're young, you can't wait to turn sixteen so you can drive. When you're sixteen, you can't wait to turn eighteen so you can go to the club. When you're in high school, you can't wait to go to college. And when you're in college, you can't wait to get a job.

"Before too long, you have nothing else to look forward to. Don't live like that. Make the most you can out of the things in life that matter."

What Coach said reminds me of John 4:35, where Jesus said, "Don't you say, 'There are still four more months, then comes the harvest'? Listen to what I'm telling you: Open your eyes and look at the fields, for they are ready for harvest."

Are our eyes open? Are we looking at the fields in front of us as opportunities to serve Christ, to be a blessing, to be the best we can possibly be? Opportunities aren't lost; they're just given away to someone else. It's up to us to take full advantage of them, not to sit around and wait. There's always something we could be doing today to give hope and promise to tomorrow.

––––––––––––

Each year during preseason camp, our entire team and staff would go to Squad Sunday at Calvary Baptist Church, located near the stadium. At this year's service, Barrett Jones talked about how hard he had worked during our run to the national championship in 2009 and how amazing it felt to hold that crystal ball over his head.

But one day, my father (bless his heart) just wanted to touch that ball—not pick it up, just touch it. When he did, his foot got caught in the tablecloth, and as he stepped away, he accidentally bumped the table leg. The crystal football rolled off, hit the floor, and shattered into a million pieces.

Of course everyone rushed to get away from it. I just went up to my dad and gave him a hug and laughed and told him everything was going to be all right. Everything turned out fine; they got the ball replaced.

But Barrett, seeing what had happened, said he thought about all the years of work he'd put into winning that trophy—how much he thought that ball meant. And now, there it was, shattered into a million pieces on the floor. He told us that in the long run, it didn't mean anything. Not a thing.

And that's true. No matter how many rings we wear or trophies we have or championships we've won, it doesn't really mean much in the context of your entire life.

During the spring before the tornado, I started to realize what really mattered. I remember sitting on my back porch thinking there must be more to life than just football. I was caught up in the wrong things. I don't know how I had gotten like this, but I had. And I knew it wasn't right.

I had seen guys who all they ever wanted was money, cars, women, and fame. That's all they ever chased, and they got it. They became first-round picks. They attained their dreams. They achieved the heights of success and everything that came along with it. But when they would come back to the football complex to visit, they were still the same guys.

We would ask them, "Man, what's it like?" And they would look at us the same way they'd looked at us the year before, when they weren't worth anything financially, and say, "It's the same, man, nothing has changed. It's not what I thought it would be."

That's a look I'll never forget. Listening to them made me realize that none of that stuff matters in the long run. Some people chase the good life and all the extras it's supposed to provide. But in the end, it doesn't mean anything. God wants us to chase after Him and what He offers.

Sitting on my back porch thinking about all of this, I asked God to change me. I wanted to be different. I didn't want to be like those guys—obtaining everything they always wanted, only to find it so much less satisfying than they'd hoped. I wanted God to help me know where real joy and fulfillment came from and how to spend my life going after those things. I was tired of just being like everyone else.

Boy, did He change my life on April 27.

CHAPTER 20

Vision or Circumstance?

LSU • November 5, 2011 • Tuscaloosa

After a week of much-needed rest, game week was finally here.

Not just any game week. *The* game week.

I guess if Alabama-LSU was the "Game of the Century," then the week before was the "Game Week of the Century." I've never seen a campus, a fan base, or for that matter a nation so jacked up about a football game.

It had all the makings of a classic battle—No. 1 LSU vs. No. 2 Alabama for what amounted to a spot in the BCS National Championship game. Tickets were going for $1,500 a pair in some places. ESPN went into overdrive the whole week, coming to town earlier than normal for its *GameDay* coverage. CBS, which had already shown our Florida game in prime time, wheeled and dealed to put the game in the 7:00 p.m. time slot.

Coach Saban told us not to pay attention to the media, but it was impossible not to. The hype for this game was everywhere, and frankly, who could resist? It gave me chills every time I saw it advertised on television. Heck, it gave me chills every time I *thought* about it.

You come to Alabama to play in big games like this. Games such as Alabama-LSU on the national stage are what you live for as a football player and a competitor.

I just wish we could have played better.

In a powerful defensive battle with each team throwing—and taking—punch after punch, LSU prevailed, 9–6, in overtime. It just wasn't our night. Four missed field goals, including one in overtime, and two costly interceptions were just too much to overcome.

Where would we go from here?

How would we bounce back from a game like this?

In a heartbroken locker room, Coach Saban laid out the situation with his classic wisdom. He said we could either let this loss define us, or we could come together and do something very special. He told us to chalk it up as a learning experience and make a commitment to each other for the rest of the season. He challenged us to forget about the loss and just focus on the Process, not the scoreboard.

That's what I had kept telling myself after the tornado. I wasn't going to be defined by the adversity; I wanted to be defined by how I responded to it. I did not want to be defined by a spring storm and the destruction it caused, the ramifications it left behind, or the losses it gave me. I never did and I never want to be.

At first, I wasn't even sure I wanted to write this book because I didn't want people to harp on my circumstance. But I did want to show how I responded after my circumstance, in hopes I could help others battle through the hardships in their own lives. I wanted people to see me living in vision. That's my story—living in vision, not circumstance.

On the Monday after the LSU loss, Damion Square, our rock-steady defensive tackle, stood up in front of the team and talked about a poster of Martin Luther King Jr. hanging in his room. On it was this quote: "The ultimate measure of a man is not where he stands in moments of comfort and convenience, but where he stands at times of challenge and controversy."

Damion knew what our team could do, and he reminded us of it after the LSU game. He knew we were better than how we had played against them, but that didn't matter. We were going to be defined by where we went from there. As the poster said, we'd be measured from that point on by how we responded to our challenge.

In vision, not circumstance.

One shining example of responding to a challenge was Quinton Dial, a key backup at defensive tackle during the 2011 season. One Sunday he asked me to go to church with him. They had asked him to speak that day. I said, "Sure, man," and I was all over it. I was the only white guy there, but I didn't care at all. I was fired up. They had great music, and everyone was excited to hear Quinton speak.

Quinton has the most soft-spoken voice I've ever heard. He began to talk about his growing up and how rebellious he was, how he stayed in trouble, and that he always felt bad for how he made his mom feel. He said he felt like he was letting her down. He prayed and asked God to help him figure out how he was supposed to live. He knew he needed to do better than this.

A few months after that, Quinton lost his mom in a house fire. But instead of rejecting God or going back to the way he'd been living, he turned to Him and relied on Him even more. Quinton is a happy man in Christ now. I'll never forget what he said that day: "Don't let where you come from determine where you're going."

Quinton had a circumstance, but he chose to live in vision.

―――――――――

Although we were committed to Coach Saban's directive to finish out the season on a positive note, we no longer had control of our own destiny. All the experts basically said the Alabama-LSU winner would play in the BCS game, while the loser would be on the outside looking in.

But in the event that somehow, someway, both Alabama and LSU got to the BCS game, I felt good about our chances after seeing one short quote from Brandon Taylor, LSU's safety, following the game.

"Alabama's a tough team," he said. "They've got good players and an outstanding coach.

"I wouldn't want to play them again."

CHAPTER 21

Believing in Yourself

Mississippi State • November 12, 2011 •
Starkville, Mississippi

Committing to finish the season on a positive note was easier said than done.

The LSU loss was a tough one to swallow. Looking at the film, we knew we were the better team. I'm not sure if we were too uptight, or if the hype got to us, or what, but we just didn't play well, primarily on the offensive side of the ball.

Regardless of the circumstances, missing four field goals in such a monumental game is what people remember the most. And believe me, no one felt worse about it than Cade Foster, who missed from 44, 50, and 52 yards. Jeremy Shelley, our short-yardage kicker, had a 49-yard attempt blocked, while each of them made one field goal—Jeremy from 34 yards and Cade from 46 yards.

Coach Saban would always tell us, "Every play has a history and a life of its own. No matter what happens on that play, you have to forget about it, good or bad, and move on to the next play. If you're focused on what you did the play before, how can you focus on the next play?"

I think this is what made Jeremy such a good kicker during his Alabama career. He put in so much preparation that when he was kicking in a game, he didn't even have to think about it. Whether he made it or missed it, he'd forget about it. He played with an even keel. He never got high off a big kick and never got low after missing one.

I tried doing my part to help keep it that way. Any time Cade or Jeremy attempted a field goal, regardless of whether they made it or not, I never treated them any different during the game. We would get to the sideline, and I would go sit on the defensive bench for a while. Only after they'd had some time to themselves would I go over and talk to them about the kick. And whether they had missed it or made it, I would still tell them to "shake it off," to focus on making the next one.

Following the LSU loss, before we even left the locker room, the specialists vowed not to change anything about our preparation or routine. We reminded ourselves that everyone has a bad night. We pledged not to think about it anymore and to go back to work on Monday with a fresh mind-set and a focus on getting better, just like we always did.

Again, easier said than done.

During the week, as we were trying to prepare for an always-tough Mississippi State team, Cade went through a difficult and trying time. I had always been there for Cade, through the good and the bad. When he was doing well, I'd hang with him so he could stay focused. And when he was down, I'd be there to pick him up a little bit. This was definitely one of those "pick up" times. He couldn't seem to shake what felt like responsibility for the loss. I simply told

Cade that everyone out there knew he was qualified for the job; everyone had seen him make those kicks hundreds of times. All the coaches, all the players, everyone had faith in him. I told him that Coach Saban wouldn't have put him out there if he didn't think he could kick. I told him he was the man for the job.

Even in his weekly press conference, Coach Saban came to the kickers' rescue, saying that the kicks would've been much more makeable had the offense not "gone backwards" on several occasions. When asked if he felt good about the psyche of the kickers, Coach said, "I do. I do. Just like I said forty years ago—'I do.'"

Funny.

But no matter what Coach said, or what I said, Cade was the one who had to believe he could bounce back. None of our encouragement meant anything if he didn't believe in himself.

I could relate to that. The days and months after the tornado were, of course, very hard for me. But as much as possible, I tried to look at it as though it was all part of God's plan. If He didn't think I could handle it, He wouldn't have put it on my shoulders.

The biggest thing I learned from my experience is this: in everything you do, do it as if it's God's plan. You never know what kind of opportunity it may lead to. You need to believe in what God can accomplish inside you as you walk through it with courage and trust and the commitment to keep doing the right things.

It really comes down to believing in yourself. Anyone can say they believe in God, which is really pretty easy. What's hard is believing in God during the hard times, believing He put you there for a reason so you can lean on Him, depend on Him, and learn from the situation. Faith is a gift He gives us to help follow Him, and we're expected to use it.

As speaker Kevin Elko told us one time, "Don't just do what your coaches tell you; believe in it." That's what I love about Elko. Everything he says about football is applicable to your life—physically, emotionally, and spiritually.

The aftermath of the LSU loss was our chance to see if we did . . . to see if we believed.

With everything we had gone through after the LSU game, we needed to turn our attention to one thing—traveling to Starkville to take on Mississippi State. In front of the second-largest crowd in stadium history, we shook off about a million raucous cowbells to win, 24–7. It was a tough game. Mississippi State was a good team that played their hearts out. We came out slow and couldn't get a rhythm, but we kept grinding and found a way.

Once again, our defense—led by Dont'a Hightower and Mark Barron—came to the rescue, holding the Bulldogs to only 131 yards. Trent Richardson's 127 rushing yards on a record 32 carries and Eddie Lacy's 96 yards led a punishing ground game.

With only two games left in the regular season, our goals became simple—first, do our jobs on the field and master the things we could control. And second, hope that other teams would stumble, something over which we had no control.

A week later, Christmas came early.

CHAPTER 22

Focus and Refocus

Georgia Southern • November 19, 2011 •
Tuscaloosa

I mentioned this earlier, but during my time at Alabama, I just loved listening to our team chaplain, Jeremiah Castille. From the time I arrived in Tuscaloosa to the time I left, there was not a day when I didn't think about something he said, or a biblical truth he expounded on, or a word of wisdom he gave us.

One such nugget was, "Winners can focus; champions can refocus."

I could probably write a book about everything I learned from Coach Castille, but the one thing he harped on every game day was "focus." He wrote it on the board every week: FOCUS—*F*ollow *O*n *C*ourse *U*ntil *S*uccessful.

At this point in the season, we weren't yet successful (by *our* definition, at least), but we knew if we kept working, kept following the Process, and kept on course, we would be successful.

Through Coach Saban's eyes, of course, being successful had nothing to do with the scoreboard, or even winning. His goal for us was to be the best players we could be. It was never about winning a national championship or even winning a game. It was about dominating the man in front of you one play at a time, and everything else will take care of itself.

I've never in my life seen someone so focused as Coach Saban. During the Georgia Southern week, when all our fans were worried about so-and-so beating so-and-so, analyzing the various scenarios that might give us a chance to sneak back into the BCS game, Coach Saban's message to us was constant:

"We can't veer off the course."

"Whenever we focus on other things, we aren't successful."

"Distractions are thieves."

"Focus on what we can control."

We were not to listen to the media, or other teams, or the fans, or our friends. All we needed to think about was playing football, staying committed to our goals, living up to the standard we'd set for ourselves.

Focus.

Another gem I learned from Coach was that you can't focus on everything at once. You can only focus on the things that are happening right now, making the *now* better. Do that, and the future will fall into place. It's all about consistency. Coach Saban repeatedly told us that if consistency were a town, it would be a ghost town—meaning that consistency is hard to maintain, and few are up to the challenge. However, consistency is what Coach Saban demanded of us. It didn't matter what you could do *one* time; it mattered what you could do *every* time. It wasn't about how fast you could do one repetition; it was about how fast you could go through an entire practice.

During practices, I loved talking to our head referee Eddie Conyers, a fixture on our practice field for more than fifty years, all the way back to the early Coach Bryant days. Eddie now has a crew that handles most of the officiating duties, so he mostly just hangs out with the players and tells stories about his life and the glory days of Alabama football.

One time he told me that Coach Bryant didn't run any kind of fancy offense; he only ran about six or seven plays. But his teams perfected those plays. He told me Coach Bryant would keep practicing those same plays over and over until they could run them without a single hitch. Eddie said, "Coach Bryant didn't run the plays until they got them right; he kept running the plays until they couldn't get them wrong."

That takes focus.

———

In our team meeting on the day before the Georgia Southern game, Coach walked in; and, like always, the room got quiet. He pulled out a sheet of paper and began to read:

> We are a team that plays for sixty minutes
> to put fear in the eyes of our opponents.
> Our goal is simple: dominate every phase
> of every game and every opponent we face.
> Our offense is unstoppable and explosive.
> Our defense is suffocating and relent-
> less. Our special teams are game changers.
> We are a family with one vision, purpose,

and attitude: to leave our opponents with
no doubt of the Bama way. Our greatest
strengths are the warriors fighting next to
us. We are a team that opponents hate to
face in the fourth quarter. When the clock
reads 00:00, five words will define us: Discipline, Effort, Commitment, Toughness,
and Pride.

He didn't need to introduce or explain what he was
reading. It was the Affirmation we'd written during camp,
listing our beliefs and standards for the upcoming season.

After finishing, Coach said, "These are your goals; this
is the standard you set for yourself. It doesn't say anything
about winning or losing in here; it talks about being the
player you want to be. Have you been living up to this?"

You could have heard a pin drop.

That Affirmation was our vision. It was something we
had written and wanted to be. It was time for us to focus on
our vision—the things we could control—instead of focusing on our circumstances.

———————

I'm not sure it's possible in college football to get four
wins in one weekend, but for us, that's just about what
happened.

I know we were supposed to be focusing on the Process,
keeping to our standard, having our minds only on Georgia
Southern. But that certainly didn't mean we didn't celebrate
when Iowa State upset No. 2 Oklahoma State on the Friday
night before our Saturday game.

I have to admit—there was probably not one Alabama player who wasn't watching the game from inside our rooms at the Hotel Capstone on campus. And when Iowa State scored the winning touchdown in the second overtime, many of the players spilled out into the hallways, hollering and high-fiving like you wouldn't believe. Just like that, probably the only team standing in the way of an Alabama-LSU rematch had bitten the dust.

The next morning on game day, in the coaches' staff meeting, word got to Coach Saban of our celebrations. He felt the urgency to talk to our team about it.

Only once, when Coach introduced U.S. Supreme Court Justice Clarence Thomas to us, had he ever spoken to us during our pregame meal. But on this day, he felt it necessary to cool our jets about what had happened the night before.

In a way that only he can deliver, Coach Saban told us to forget what had happened the night before and to be concerned only about our game that day against Georgia Southern. He said if we lost—like Oklahoma State had lost the night before—then we'd be the victim of some other team's celebration. He definitely got our attention.

Although the game was never really in doubt, Georgia Southern sure came to play. Using an option-style offense, they racked up more than 300 yards rushing on us—by far the most of any opponent we faced in 2011. Still, we ended up winning, 45–21.

And from there, the good news kept coming.

Although not as significant as Iowa State's shocker over Oklahoma State on Friday night, our other two "victories" that weekend were Baylor's win over No. 5 Oklahoma and Southern Cal's victory over No. 4 Oregon. Even though these two teams were behind us in the polls, the more losses they had, the more Alabama and LSU could distance themselves from the rest of the pack.

By Sunday night, our wishes had been granted. Standing atop the BCS poll stood two SEC teams—Alabama at No. 2 and LSU at No. 1.

And only one game remained on our schedule.

Yes, that one.

It was "Never Again" time.

CHAPTER 23

Finish

Auburn • November 26, 2011 •
Auburn, Alabama

For an entire year—from the time Auburn rallied from 24 points down in 2010 to beat us 28–27 in Tuscaloosa—the "Never Again" reminders were everywhere.

"Never Again" in the weight room.

"Never Again" in the locker room.

"Never Again" in the football offices.

We even had "Never Again" posters in our houses.

And of course, Coach Cochran couldn't go a day without yelling it, over and over.

"Never Again."

Our trip to Auburn for the season finale served a dual purpose. First, we had to do everything we could do to show the nation that we deserved to be in the national championship game. We wanted to leave it all on the line.

Second, we wanted to make sure that "Never Again" meant . . . well, you know.

Our attitude going into this game was simple: We will not be denied what we want. And this week, all we wanted was to beat Auburn. All those affirmations we had made before the season, we wanted to take them out on our biggest rival. We wanted to finish what we started.

Everything you do in life is about the finish. The finish line never comes *to* you; you run *through* it. We had goals as a team, but we had not yet seen them through. Furthermore, we had not yet played our best game of the season.

Finishing and reaching goals are constant themes throughout the New Testament. One of my favorite verses is 1 Corinthians 9:24, which says, "Don't you know that the runners in a stadium all race, but only one receives the prize? Run in such a way to win the prize."

At the end of the day, with Trent Richardson doing the running, the prize was ours.

In our 42–14 victory, Trent galloped for a career-high 203 yards, which amounted to 63 more yards than the entire Auburn team, whose only scores came on a recovered fumble in the end zone and a kickoff return to open the second half. Besides Trent's heroics, A. J. McCarron and tight end Brad Smelley stood out with solid performances.

Similar to our game against Auburn the year before, we jumped out to a big lead in this one. By halftime, we had an eerily familiar 24–7 lead, the same as in 2010.

The problem in the 2010 game? We didn't finish. We didn't do what was needed to close the deal, even after holding such a large halftime lead. We weren't about to let it happen again.

This time, a year later, we finished what we started.

I loved what Coach Saban said to the media after the game: "Our goal today was to play our best football game and to play the best that we could play. It wasn't perfect, but it was one of the better games we have played on offense and defense. It was really OK on special teams except for kickoff returns. I don't think there are words to describe how proud I am of our players."

Notice he didn't say our goal was to *win* the game but to play our *best* game. That is his philosophy and therefore his team's philosophy.

And that is how you finish strong.

———————

Following the game, there was no question in our minds we deserved a spot in the BCS National Championship Game. But until the votes were in and the computers crunched their numbers, we'd be left guessing.

Needless to say, a suspenseful week lay ahead.

CHAPTER 24

The Setup

BCS National Championship Game •
January 9, 2012 • New Orleans, Louisiana

Following our win over Auburn, the speculation all week long—even from the national media—seemed to indicate that Alabama and LSU would indeed meet again, this time for the BCS title.

As far as we were concerned, only two games of significant importance were left on the college football landscape—LSU vs. Georgia in the SEC Championship Game on December 3 and, later that night, Oklahoma-Oklahoma State. In Atlanta, LSU scored 35 second-half points to easily defeat Georgia, 42–10, and secure its spot in the BCS game.

That evening's late game in Stillwater, however, gave us cause for concern. Oklahoma State soundly defeated No. 9 Oklahoma, 44–10, leading many people to believe the No. 3 Cowboys could vault past us in the BCS standings.

But despite Oklahoma State's win—and their subsequent campaign for a berth in the game—the BCS standings revealed LSU and Alabama as the top two teams. Official word of the pairing came to us via the *BCS Selection Show* on ESPN at our annual football banquet in Birmingham. Although the news was exactly what we were hoping for, we kept our emotions in check. We knew we had a job to do.

The final margin was close in the rankings between us and Oklahoma State, but in the end the BCS got what it wanted—the nation's two best teams playing for the national title.

With our spirits rejuvenated, the first couple of weeks of December were spent on conditioning, working out, studying, taking final exams, and getting some rest. I'm sure our coaches were working night and day on LSU, but for us it wasn't yet time.

In the week following our football banquet, I had the honor of accompanying Coach Saban and several of my teammates to Orlando for the Home Depot College Football Awards show. There I was, just a long snapper, hanging out at Disney World with all the stars—Andrew Luck, Robert Griffin III (the eventual Heisman Trophy winner), Tyrann Mathieu, and Erin Andrews from ESPN, among others. It was fun, of course, but I'll say this: those folks weren't any cooler than my teammates.

At the awards show, televised live on ESPN, I accepted the Disney Spirit Award on behalf of the Alabama football team. Handed out each year since 1996, the award goes to college football's most inspirational player, team, or figure.

The award didn't represent me or anything I did; it represented our team, our University, and the Tuscaloosa community. I wasn't the only one who had gone through a tragedy. A lot of people had experienced the same thing I had. I wasn't crazy about how the spotlight was on me in particular, but I was proud to stand there for my team and my town.

Since April 27, everyone had reached out and pulled together as a family in the face of this tragedy. Yes, the tornado had taken so much from us, but with a spirit of hope and a lot of hard work, we had rallied together and overcome our challenges—not for this kind of recognition but just to be a blessing in other people's lives.

We hoped a national title might be another one of those blessings we could give them.

On Monday, December 19, we gathered back on campus to start preparations for the "Rematch of the Century." I know most folks outside the South weren't particularly excited about watching two SEC teams play in the title game, but it's not like we had concocted the game out of thin air. Under the policies and formulas set by the BCS, Alabama and LSU had earned their way to New Orleans.

During our first team meeting, Coach Saban told us we weren't going to do anything different for this game. We weren't going to prepare any different or change our game plan from the first LSU game; we were just going to execute the same game plan better.

A lot of people asked me if the kickers, who had missed four field goals in the first game, were going to alter how they prepared for this game. I told them we were going to do the same thing we always did. I reminded them what Coach always said: "Every play has a history and a life of its own." As far as we were concerned, those missed kicks were history.

A few days before we left for New Orleans, Kevin Elko came and spoke to us. I'd heard Elko speak dozens of times at various places, but what he told us that night was on another level. Incredible. The images he laid on our minds will never go away.

He started talking about the biblical story of Lazarus from the book of John and how Jesus wept because He felt the pain that Lazarus's family felt. Elko related it to the first LSU game, where we had felt such a deep level of pain following the loss. He mentally took us back into that postgame locker room and asked us to remember the pain and the bad taste in our mouth. And sure enough, everyone started remembering.

Trust me, none of us wanted to feel that pain again. And we didn't want our brothers to feel it either. In an emotionally charged team meeting room, we all made a promise to each other that we were going to do everything we could do to make sure our teammates didn't feel that pain again.

Elko then began to talk about how this whole game was a *setup*—the whole season, the first loss to LSU, all the other teams losing in order for us to have a shot. It was all just a *setup*—a chance for everyone to see that we were more than just a good football team, that we were a family, a family that cared for our community and put a whole city on our back when it needed us the most. This game was a setup for everyone in the country to see that.

Furthermore, it was a setup for LSU. We had set them up into thinking they were the better team, when in reality, we all knew we had the better team.

It was a setup. A setup. The whole thing was a setup.

We got it.

So, yes, we went down to New Orleans and participated in the bowl activities they'd prepared for us, all the dinners and such, but everyone treated it like a business trip. Everyone was there on a mission—to carry out the setup. It was a great environment to be around.

In a team meeting a few days before the game, you could tell Coach Saban had this sense of peace over him. He could see that we were focused and prepared. He said, "I know what you want, guys. You've put in the work and have done what it takes. We're going to get what you want, I promise."

Hearing his confidence gave me chills. There was just a feeling of complete calm over everyone after that. We conducted our walk-through in the Saints practice facility, and everyone executed everything perfectly. It was a beautiful practice.

Leading up to the game, we all knew we had it. It didn't have anything to do with LSU; it was all about us and what we did. We knew we couldn't fail. We were going to give our teammates the best opportunity to do something significant.

During our pregame warm-ups in the Superdome, all the players were telling each other, "It's just a setup; it's just a setup; it's just a setup." We had all bought into Elko's setup strategy. And after warm-ups, as we headed back into the locker room, Courtney Upshaw walked up to me and said, "I love you, bro. This one's for you."

No—this one was for Alabama.

How do I adequately express how much our 21–0 win meant to us? To our school? To our community? To our state?

Eight and a half months earlier, as 12 percent of Tuscaloosa lay in ruins, as the University's final exams were cancelled and graduation postponed, could anyone have guessed that we would bring home the BCS crystal? I don't think so.

Where do I begin giving the credit to our on-the-field heroes in this game? I'll start with Courtney Upshaw, who had told me, "This one's for you." All he did was win defensive MVP honors with seven tackles and a sack.

Courtney, along with Mark Barron and Dont'a Hightower, took charge of the defense during all our bowl practices and right through the final tick of the clock. They just had that look in their eyes. There was no way they were going to be denied. Even linebacker Jerrell Harris, a part-time starter who'd been averaging about two tackles a game, ended up with seven tackles and constantly disrupted LSU's option plays. All in all, we held LSU to 92 yards total offense and five first downs, a staggering statistic.

I know there have been great defenses in years past at Alabama, and I know there will be great defenses in years to come, but I'll put our 2011 squad up against any of them. Statistically, we finished first in the nation in total defense, pass efficiency, scoring defense, rushing defense, and pass defense. I'm glad those guys were on my side.

Offensively, A. J. McCarron became a man that day. Named offensive MVP, he picked apart LSU's defense and finished the game 23 of 34 for 234 yards. His strikes to seven different receivers kept LSU off balance all night long.

Trent Richardson, even in somewhat of a decoy role, was a workhorse—as usual—rushing for 96 yards on 20 carries and our only touchdown.

And then, there's my brother Jeremy Shelley, who, along with Cade Foster, had been so maligned after the first LSU game. All Jeremy did was tie an all-time bowl record with five made field goals and set an all-time bowl record with seven attempts.

In comparing this LSU game to our November 5 game in Tuscaloosa, our offense in this one was able to penetrate much farther into LSU territory, which obviously made all the difference in the world—and the outcome. In the first game, we missed field goals of 44, 50, 49, and 52 yards, an average of almost 49 yards per kick. In the BCS game, Jeremy *made* field goals of 23, 34, 41, 35, and 44 yards, a 35-yard average. Our offense, though unable to punch it in against a very good LSU defense until Trent's late touchdown, gave our kicking game just the boost it needed.

I can't tell you how proud I was of Jeremy and Cade for hanging in there through a difficult time following the first LSU game. Redemption was sweet. The setup was complete.

And we were champions.

CHAPTER 25

Back-to-Back

The 2012 Season

Our journey in repeating as national champions in 2012 didn't start when we opened fall camp in early August. It started about twenty-four hours after winning the 2011 title.

Everyone was on another planet after our victory over LSU in the BCS title game. We were obviously very excited and completely soaking in the moment. And while Coach Saban was equally ecstatic about our accomplishment, it didn't keep him from sticking to his twenty-four-hour rule.

The next morning, he was back on the Process.

The game had been played on a Monday night. And less than eighteen hours later, on Tuesday afternoon, we flew home to Tuscaloosa. Not missing a beat, Coach Saban and the other coaches got right back to work. You would never have known we had just won a national championship.

On Wednesday—two days after the win—we had a team meeting. Coach said he was very proud of everything we had accomplished. He said that no one could ever take away from us what we'd done. He said we had accomplished something the richest man in the world couldn't buy, and we had done it together.

But then he talked about the difference between being good and being great, how no team had ever won back-to-back national titles in the BCS era. Coach said that the hardest thing to do in sports is to refuse complacency—to be the best you can be two times in a row.

And, he said, he wanted our football team to do it.

But in order for us to win back-to-back titles, it was going to take all of us buying back into the Process—not focusing on the championship we'd just won but focusing instead on what it took to win. Not focusing on winning but on what it takes to get there.

Coach asked us if we were in.

And everyone agreed: yes, we wanted to do this again.

During the off-season, we worked harder than ever. Our Fourth Quarter conditioning program was tougher than it had ever been. Our summer workouts and runs were tougher too. And our coaches were more intense than ever. Yes, we wanted to go back-to-back, but we never let ourselves *talk* about going back-to-back. We just talked about what this year's team wanted to accomplish. Just as in 2011, this team needed to create a new identity, and it was going to have to start in camp.

Everything went back to the Process. Preseason camp was set up the same way as before—the practices, the workouts, the schedule, even having Kevin Elko come to speak to us. And he brought us a great message again.

He opened up talking about Jesus' first miracle of turning water into wine, recorded in the second chapter of John. Jesus was at a wedding where the hosts ran out of wine. When informed of this by His mother, Mary, He told the servants to fill six stone jars with water. As they were carrying the jars to the head steward, the water turned into wine.

Elko challenged us with a new theme for the season: *"Keep carrying the water until it turns to wine."*

We started the year strong at Cowboys Stadium in Dallas with a convincing 41–14 win over Michigan. After that game, I knew we had another good team and were going to have a chance to do great things.

But we knew we had to keep fighting through adversity, just like in 2011. Coach Saban told us you never know what kind of boxer someone is until he gets hit in the mouth. We got hit in the mouth a few times during the season, but through our adversity we kept telling each other: *"Keep carrying the water until it turns to wine."*

One of those "hit in the mouth" games was in Baton Rouge against LSU. Going in, we were 8–0, ranked No. 1, and had outscored our opponents 325–65. But after watching our 14–3 halftime lead slowly evaporate, we found ourselves down 17–14 in the fourth quarter. Two strong defensive stands saved the day for us, the last of which gave us the ball on our 28-yard line with 1:34 remaining. With nerves of steel, A. J. piloted a furious five-play, 72-yard scoring drive to put us ahead for good, 21–17. Never have I been on a sideline with so much emotion. I know everybody made a big deal about A. J. crying, but those were tears of victory.

In our postgame locker room, we cranked up the biggest celebration I've ever been a part of. Despite our excitement, though, Coach quickly brought us back down to earth. He told us we weren't through yet. We hadn't accomplished what we came to accomplish.

In other words, we had to keep carrying the water.

The next week in Tuscaloosa, we caught a buzz saw in Texas A&M and Johnny Manziel. Before we knew what hit us, we were down, 20–0. We fought back and had a couple of chances to win in the end but just couldn't pull it off. Final score: Texas A&M 29, Alabama 24.

After the loss, Coach Saban looked at the seniors and said, "Where do we go from here?" He didn't want to hear our circumstance; he wanted to hear our vision. I knew exactly what he wanted to hear, so I stole his speech from the year before and repeated it to the team. I told everyone we could still accomplish great things, but we had to do it together. We had to keep carrying the water.

So we kept fighting. "Never Again" rang true again as we easily beat Auburn, 49–0. Then in about as exciting a game as you'd ever want to see, we came back to defeat Georgia, 32–28, for the SEC championship.

But beating Georgia wasn't enough. We had to keep carrying the water.

Next up was Notre Dame in the BCS National Championship Game in Miami. Although after watching weeks of film on the Irish and believing from the very first day we'd win, it wasn't until right before the game that I was absolutely, positively certain.

During pregame, when our specialists and Notre Dame's specialists were warming up on the field, the customary small talk began. And I could tell right away—their specialists were in awe. Certainly not of me but of our team. They were in awe of Alabama. They were thinking, like, *Whoa, we're playing Alabama!* They'd come up to me and say, like, "Hey, man, good luck to you," and "Congratulations on going to the Senior Bowl."

I had never before heard that from anybody we were about to play. It was just different. And since we'd been in a game of such magnitude before and Notre Dame hadn't—or at least, not in a while—I sensed right then it would be a long night for them. And of course, it was.

What an amazing way to end my college career—going out on top with my brothers, preparing to launch into the next phase of my life knowing what it means to set a standard for myself and the people around me, to work the Process that leads to success, to live with discipline, toughness, perseverance, and pride. To know as a twenty-three-year-old young man how to live in vision instead of circumstance. And to be a positive blessing to others, even in the midst of the toughest adversity.

That's what I've learned. That's who I am.

And I will never stop being thankful for it.

Following our 42–14 victory over the Irish, I sent Elko a simple text:

The water is now wine. Thanks.

A Field's Memories

Today, standing at the end of 25th Street, gazing around at a world gone by, the memories roam in my mind.

In one flash, I'm in the massive eighteen-acre field full of pecan, pine, and oak trees, leaving all my cares behind, watching Josey and B race after my golf balls. In another, all I see are those same trees ripped out of the soil or snapped in half like toothpicks.

In another image, there's my quaint little house, the perfect abode for three college kids. Then, with a blink of the eye, I see it pushed across the street in a ten-foot-high pile of twisted lumber, shattered bricks, and crumbled drywall. Buried deep within the carnage is every possession I own, except my Jeep and the clothes on my back.

In yet another flash, I see the backside of the beautiful Glendale Gardens neighborhood, with its pristine ivy-covered fences and walls, crepe myrtles, fountains, birdbaths, and flowers exploding in color. Then, as far as I can see, is a row of backyards, flattened like pancakes. One house is totally missing, whisked away from its foundation, as if it had never been there.

Today, though, I see something different.

I see a neighborhood living in vision, not circumstance.

Thanks to the surrounding residents—especially the Prices and Johnsons, who, between their families, own twelve acres of the eighteen-acre field—my old neighborhood is making a comeback.

On the piece of land where my house once stood, there's a new house with college kids living in it. To the left, a vacant lot is all that remains of the house with the basement—the one we thought about running into if a tornado ever came our way. And to the right is another vacant lot with two large tree stumps from my neighbor's pine trees, the ones he was sure were going to fall on his house. In an odd twist, those trees actually survived the storm; he had them cut down later. I think that's a pretty neat story in itself. I find peace in that.

The homes in Glendale Gardens, always classy in style, now look twenty years younger. Those owners—a proud, determined bunch—have been leaders in the "T-Town, Never Down" effort, which has caught on throughout Tuscaloosa.

And then, there's the field, in which I now find solace. I think back to that day and where I could've been, maybe even should've been, and where I am now.

Down the field's west side, just behind the Glendale Gardens homes, are twenty-eight crepe myrtles, carefully planted by Rick Price and spaced in perfect proportion, all the way up to his house on Hillcrest. They're decades away from replacing the massive trees that were once there, but one day they'll provide nice shade to those Glendale Gardens backyards.

In the corner of the field closest to where the remnants of my house were, not far from where I was found following the tornado, is the memorial to Ashley. Next to it is the one for Josey and B. Keeping the memorials tidy has become a personal crusade for Jim and Mary Jean Johnson, especially Mary Jean, who walks back there every day to, as she says, "take care of my babies." Her "babies" are all the plants and trees that have been planted in honor of, or in memory of, those affected by the tornado.

Surrounding the memorials are rosebushes named for Ashley, Josey, B, Ashley's parents David and Darlene, Ashley's grandparents, and even me. A small cedar tree, planted by Ashley's parents, is decorated every Christmas.

One time I asked Mary Jean what she thinks about when she goes back there with her water hose in hand. "Talking to them has become my cathedral," she said. "I ask the plants and bushes, 'How're you doing? You're looking good today.'"

Here's a lady who lost fifty-one gorgeous trees in her portion of the field, yet she's back there every day, taking care of her new "babies." Mary Jean had a circumstance, just like everyone else in this world. But she's chosen instead to live in vision.

A vision as bright as the roses blooming in a field where Ashley will never be forgotten.

Afterword

by Kevin Elko

Every day you see thousands of objects, but you *notice* seeing only a few. Even though you see many *different* things, you are only aware of seeing the same things. For example, have you noticed how the day after you buy a new car, you start seeing that same car everywhere, passing you on the road and in parking lots? This is called *inattentional blindness,* a term meaning that we are blind to those things we do not give attention to, while the things we *do* give attention to, we see.

This phenomenon is the result of a part of the brain called the Reticular Activation System, which sits at the back of the head. This system controls what we notice, be it constant curses (negativity) or constant blessings (positivity). In other words, we can actually control what we see and notice.

Because of this system, most people—after experiencing a mishap, catastrophe, or loss of some kind—*see* only loss and catastrophe. Their attention goes to these events, and like the new car, they see the loss and awfulness everywhere. Some spend the rest of their lives noticing the wrong and the evil, meditating on negativity for years.

Two things control our Reticular Activation System: what we feed our minds and what we say. In other words, if we *feed* ourselves garbage, and if we *speak* garbage, then we *see* garbage. As Moses said in Deuteronomy, God has placed in front of us life and death, so choose life (see Deut. 30:19). But choosing life is a daily choice. It is intentional living, including what you read, watch, say (i.e., the conversations you step into and, most importantly, that you speak). Life and death is in the tongue, the Bible says. Some speak life and some speak death. Feed it and then see it; speak it and then see it.

Although this concept sounds simple, it is much too important to let happen by chance. If our lives are to abound, we must choose what words we say and what we are going to feed. We must feed ourselves good works and speak of good things. We must choose what we are going to see before we see it.

In these pages, you've read of Carson Tinker, of loss, and of his view of life. His world shows images of tornadoes and a broken body, but he saw life because he chose to. He gave his attention to life—not living in circumstance but rather in vision. This book demonstrates that we are not born winners or born losers, but we are born choosers—God has given us dominion.

A prominent psychiatrist said, if you are hurting, go find someone else who is hurting and help that person. Carson Tinker's Reticular Activation System "speaks" to him that way, saying, "I'm not looking for blessings to come into my life, but I am looking to be a blessing in someone else's life." Either by helping families rebuild their homes or build their *first* home, Carson looks for someone else to uplift every day. When a sign fell on a little boy in the Birmingham airport and killed him, Carson visited the boy's brother in the hospital. There are many of these stories. In fact, I believe Carson Tinker is responsible for Alabama's 2011 and 2012 national championships because his spirit ran throughout the Crimson Tide so that the entire team had the focus of being a blessing for others. This kind of team can be unstoppable.

I have worked with a number of Hall of Fame athletes from many sports, but my favorite is Carson Tinker—for one reason: he is not looking for blessings to come into his life but rather to *be* a blessing.

I hope this book helps you improve your eyesight—to see good and to choose life, no matter what. I hope it helps you become what you, your family, and the world need right now: another blessing. I love being around Carson Tinker because attitudes are contagious, and his is worth catching.

Kevin Elko, Performance Consultant
"Head" Coach, Alabama Crimson Tide

Acknowledgments

In looking back over my days, weeks, and months since April 27, 2011, I have so many people to thank for playing a monumental part in my recovery—physically, emotionally, mentally, and spiritually. Even the smallest things felt enormous. From the bottom of my heart, thank you.

First and foremost, to my parents Carlton and Debbie Tinker, and my grandparents, Jim and Deanna Cartledge and Jean and Tommy Anderson, who have stood by me from day one. They have always been, and will forever be, a lasting inspiration to me.

I thank Dr. Thom Rainer of LifeWay Christian Resources and Tommy Ford with the Alabama Athletics Department for making this book possible—Dr. Rainer for his foresight in thinking that I indeed had a story to tell and Tommy for assisting me in putting all of my thoughts and fragments together on paper. More than two years in the making, I hope this book is as much of a blessing to you as it has been to me.

I also want to thank Payton Holley, Juli and Clay Carter, Gary Cramer, Siran Stacy, Kim Lancaster, Colin Gallagher, Spencer Whitfield, Parker Stinnett, Bob White, Joe Judge, Dave Blalock, Dr. Michael Beckenstein, Dr. Jimmy Robinson, Dr. Lyle Cain, Dr. Elwin Crawford, Jeff Allen,

Bill McDonald, Kirk Kaps, Kent Gidley, Amelia Brackin, and especially Ginger Gilmore.

A special debt of gratitude goes to Jim and Mary Jean Johnson, who to this day so faithfully keep watch over the field and the memorials.

To our head coach Nick Saban and, as we call him, our "head" coach Kevin Elko, I thank you for writing the foreword and the afterword, respectively, and for being there for me throughout this journey. Thanks, too, to all our assistant coaches and football staff members for their constant encouragement.

Thank you to Michael Pope and David Sumrall, my high school friends and teammates from Murfreesboro, Tennessee, who immediately came to Birmingham to help me navigate those first days at home. You will always be brothers to me.

To Annie Bates, an amazingly selfless and genuine person whose love supported me through a very difficult time. I look forward to our journey and all that God has planned for us.

Foundation Page

The purpose of the *Be a Blessing Foundation* is:

> To be a blessing to individuals and families that are affected by circumstance and help them with the resources we have, financially or spiritually, to live in vision.

Financial gifts to the *Be a Blessing Foundation* may be sent to:

Be a Blessing Foundation
P. O. Box 26372
Birmingham, AL 35260

www.beablessingnow.com